ELECTRIC BASS GUITAR

Revised Edition

Edited by Andy Doerschuk

The Guitar Player Basic Library

From the editors of Guitar Player and
Bass Player magazines.

GPI BOOKS

Director
Alan Rinzler

Editor:
Electric Bass Guitar, Revised Edition
Andy Doerschuk

Art Director
Paul Haggard

General Manager
Judie Eremo

Art Assistant
Robert Stockwell Jr.

GPI PUBLICATIONS

President/Publisher
Jim Crockett

Executive Vice President
Don Menn

Corporate Art Director
Wales Christian Ledgerwood

Editor: Guitar Player
Tom Wheeler

Editor: Bass Player
Andy Doerschuk

Production
Cheryl Matthews (Director)
Joyce Phillips (Assistant Director)
Andrew Gordon, Gail M. Hall, Joe Verri

Typesetting
Leslie K. Bartz (Director)
Pat Gates, June Ramirez

Order Processing
Rekha Shah
Lynne Whitlach

Special Thanks To
Guitar Center, San Jose, CA
World of Music, Cupertino, CA

Photo Credits
Cover: Paul Haggard
Ron Delany: 113
Paul Haggard: 1, 9, 21, 49, 115.
Mark MacLaren: 32 (all photos), 33 (all photos).
Ebet Roberts: 44 (all photos), 47 (all photos).
Robert Stockwell Jr.: 29, 49, 73, 91.

ISBN: 088188-907-5

Contents

Introduction

Guitar Player magazine introduced its *Basic Library* back in 1983 to provide musicians with valuable columns, private lessons, and hard-to-find features in a permanent form—preserved and organized, redesigned and updated.

The first edition of *ELECTRIC BASS GUITAR* was a practical introduction to the technique and art of playing electric bass. This revised edition combines those basics with fresh new concepts and techniques drawn from recent issues of *Guitar Player* magazine and GPI Special Editions' *Bass Player* magazine.

Many great bassists are represented in these pages, including Stanley Clarke, Jeff Berlin, Billy Sheehan, Bunny Brunel, Nathan East, Jimmy Haslip, Jerry Jemmott, Herb Mickman, and Carol Kaye. Plus, the techniques of such innovative bassists as Doug Wimbish and Stuart Hamm are analyzed in detail.

ELECTRIC BASS GUITAR does not offer everything there is to know about the art of electric bass. Consequently many suggestions for further study are offered throughout. Our hope is that the information in this book will further propel you toward your current and future goals as a bass player and as a musician.

Andy Doerschuk

Chapter 1:
Getting Started

Getting Started

Choosing A Bass Guitar

Guitar Player magazine June 1983

There are three points I feel are important in the choice of a bass. The first is to buy a name brand. This will be helpful should you "outgrow" the bass and want to trade it or sell it later. The second point is to buy a solidbody if at all possible. Hollow bodies have almost become extinct (mostly because they were more prone to feedback and strange tones), but there are still some around. The third point is to buy the best bass you can afford. It's usually a good idea to buy a better bass and a cheaper amp if you're just starting out. The amp will be used mostly for practice in the beginning, so you probably won't need a very big and powerful amp. Later on, you can save for a better one for gigs, and use the old one for practice. Purchasing a used amp can help make the better bass more affordable.

Naturally, different people have different needs. For instance, a ten-year old beginner should probably get a short-scale bass such as a Fender Mustang of Musicmaster. Later on, the bass could be modified (hotter pick-ups, more massive bridge, etc.). A player who is over five feet tall should be able to play a long-scale instrument quite comfortably. There are many good brands to choose from. For the most part, these cost anywhere from $350 to $1,000.

In the last several years, there have been great improvements in electric basses, and extra electronics have been built into many instruments. The more expensive basses often feature such circuitry, and because these instruments are not always mass produced, they may not be available in every music store. The ones in this category that have impressed me are made by Steinberger, Alembic, and Ken Smith. Some of these can cost as much as $6,000—not within the means of every bassist. Whether a bass is expensive or not, though, always check to see if you need all the features present on it.

When buying a bass, try to check the neck adjustment to see if there is a warp in the fingerboard. In some cases, this can be done simply by looking down the neck from the nut to the bridge. Fret buzz in localized sections of the neck can also point to warpage. Small warps can usually be corrected by adjusting the truss rod. If you don't know too much about basses, look the salesman in the eye and ask, "How's the neck adjustment? Can you check it for me?" Most likely, you'll receive an honest answer, and if there is any problem, he will correct it.

Very often, the strings on a new or used bass are not the best, especially if the instrument is out on the sales floor where it is played regularly. If the strings seem dead or lifeless, you may ask the salesman to throw in a new set of good strings. I stay away from round-wound strings as they tend to wear grooves in the frets faster than flatwounds, in turn causing buzzes. (Some bassists prefer roundwound for their brighter sound; if you choose them, beware of potential perils.)

Many stores will try to sell a hard-shell case. I feel that you may be better off with a soft, padded gig bag. First of all, a gig bag is lighter; second, it offers good protection; third it is much easier to handle. I even take my bass on a plane, with it hanging in a garment bag, which I place in the carry-on luggage closet. If you plan to buy other accessories, the time when you purchase your bass is a good one because you may be able to get a package deal (bass, amp, case, cord, etc.).

If you decide to buy from a pawnshop or a private party, you are taking a risk, since there are no guarantees. In such situations, be sure to try out the instrument for a few minutes. Look for worn frets, a warped neck, and electronic problems. If you lack experience, take an experienced bassist with you so that you won't get a bad deal. Don't be afraid to bargain for a lower price, either.

By Herb Mickman

A Brief Introduction To The Bass

Guitar Player **magazine September 1973**

The bass guitar's four strings are tuned, from the fourth to the first (thickest to thinnest) strings, E, A, D and G. To tune the bass with a guitarist, it is easiest to start by tuning your G string to the sound of a guitarist playing a G (third fret) on the sixth string (low E).

Music notation for the bass is always written an octave higher than the actual sound. This system was initiated to simplify the reading of bass notes.

Probably the best way to start playing is working through scales. Playing scales not only gives added strength to your fingers, but also gives you a good idea as to what notes are available to play in what keys.

One thing you should concentrate on in beginning the bass, is your right hand (for right-handers) technique. Far too many beginning bassists have a tendency to pick the strings with their thumb. If you plan to use your fingers, you should start now by alternating your index and middle fingers (right hand) whether playing scales or compositions. Using the first two fingers of your right hand now will eliminate the problem of changing from thumb to this technique later on. Alternating these two fingers will give you more efficiency and greater speed.

If you plan to use a pick on the bass, you should start now by alternating your picking strokes, up-down, as opposed to a one-direction picking stroke. Later on, you will have the option of using the all-down strokes or all up-strokes, but in the long run, it is easier to first learn an up-down alternating stroke before you get hooked on the "all-down" stroke and it becomes a habit that can be hard to break.

The A major scale includes the notes: *A, B, C♯, D, E, F♯, G♯* and *A* again. Looking at Figure 1, you will note a definite pattern to this scale.

Figure 1.

The fingering pattern for major scales is within a four-fret range. To play a major scale in any key, simply find the note (tonic) with the same name as the key selected on the low E (fourth) string of the bass and start from there, using the following four-fret range pattern: 2, 4; move up to the A string, 1, 2, 4,; move up to the D string, 1, 3, and 4. See Figure 2.

Figure 2.

You can see this pattern in the A major scale, as seen in Figure 1; or, for example, if you wanted to play a D major scale, you would first find D on the low E string of the bass. Since D on the fourth string occurs at the 10th fret, you would first depress that position. Then you would move up two frets (12th fret) for the second note of that scale. You would then move up to the A string and depress the third string at the 9th fret, then the 10th fret, the 12th, etc. The essential point being to follow the pattern as given in Figure 2.

The following is a shuffle bass pattern which works for many differnt types of blues. If you have a guitarist handy, have him play the guitar part, while you run through the bass part, so that you can get an idea as to what the feel of bass playing is.

The following rhythm arrangement is written in tablature and standard "bass clef" notation for the bass. In the tablature system, the four lines represent the strings of the bass, the bottom line is the low E string and the top line represents the G string. The numbers placed on the lines represent the frets at which you should depress the strings with your left-hand (for right-handers).

By Michael Brooks

"Bouncin' Blues Shuffle In A"

Productive Bass Lessons

Guitar Player magazine   March 1978

Do you remember the first time you picked up an electric bass and tried to play a few notes? Chances are you were able to get a decent sound on it within a few minutes. This is why perhaps 90 percent of all electric bass players teach themselves, and it's part of the reason that the bass is so popular. By comparison, other instruments such as the trumpet, violin, and oboe are much more difficult to learn, and it usually takes years of study to get a good tone.

The advantages to teaching yourself include avoiding the expense of lessons, and you gain a feeling of accomplishment. The disadvantages are that many self-taught players get into bad *physical* habits and often never develop the reading ability that is usually achieved through lessons. Teaching yourself to play is often the hard way, since it is sometimes very difficult to find out a lot of information on your own, and you may have to experiment for years to find what works best.

Recently, a knowledgeable bassist/teacher and I were discussing some of the aspects of teaching the electric bass. We both recalled our own beginnings as teenagers: We wanted to be able to do it all after two lessons. Today's young players aren't too much different, except that certain standards for an electric bassist are higher in the last ten years. More is expected of a bass player in rock, fusion, and jazz idioms. Now bass players can *really* solo.

I recalled an impatient gentleman who had called me for some lessons. What he really wanted was to be shown some licks he could play right away. He was unaware of his problems: a very crude playing technique, a limited knowledge of the fingerboard, an undeveloped ear, and an unsettled sense of time. He had been playing for only a year, but he thought he was a genius because he could get through a few licks with an aggressive flair. In the hour we spent, he gave me the hardest time I have ever had with a new student. He wouldn't let me teach him, guide him to an easier way to do things. He didn't want to take my advice about improving his technique or learning how to read music, nor would he try any ear-developing concepts. He approached the bass like an athlete watching someone else play. He produced notes, but had no idea what they were and which chords they related to. Very often I see students approaching the bass without any idea of how much practice time it takes to become a skillful accompanist and improviser. They are not realistic.

I've outlined some ideas that I feel will help you get the most out of bass lessons if you really want help. First, try to find a professional bassist who reads bass clef. You will learn the most from an organized player who has a method—starting with reading music and learning the fingerboard from bottom to top. Avoid the guitarist who also plays bass as a sideline and only shows you licks.

The next points are extremely important: Make an appointment and be there on time. This sounds easy, but a lot of people have problems keeping an appointment, and it is very frustrating to a professional player to be stood up. If you can't be there, simply call and cancel the lesson.

Next, be open to advice and follow it. The teacher obviously has more insight into the problems of playing the bass. Make sure you understand what concepts are being discussed, and follow them. Progress will come only from you putting in practice time on the instrument. You will have to set time aside each day to work on specific skills. Be sure you're in a well-lighted and quiet area so that you can concentrate. Try to spend a minimum of one hour a day. Some of my students have put in three, four, and five hours a day and have made incredible progress. Take a break each hour to give your brain and hands a rest.

To practice correctly, you will need a metronome, which will help steady your sense of time, and it's a great tool for checking your progress. Get an AC- or battery-operated one if possible.

The best way to get your money's worth out of the lesson is to come prepared. If you've really put in practice time, then you will make progress. Otherwise it is a waste of the teacher's time and your money. It's better to call and change the lesson time than to come in and be told to do everything over again. If the teacher gives out materials to be memorized, keep checking to be sure that you haven't made a mistake and practiced wrong all week.

You should be aware that the good player is not always a good teacher. Teaching takes some insight into problems, a sense of organization, a desire to help, and patience. Very often the teacher cannot get excited about your playing if you haven't put in practice time on your bass. After all, teachers have egos, too. They want to see some results for their efforts.

Where should you look for an organized teacher? Call the Musician's Union, and ask to speak to a business agent. Or alternatively, look in the Yellow Pages of the phone book under "Musical Instruments—Instruction." Also ask friends and other bass players, or call the office of a symphony orchestra in your area, and try to get the contractor's name; ask him or her if any of the bassists teach. Remember you'll only get out of the bass what you put into it.

By Herb Mickman

Music College And Bass Proficiency

An overwhelming majority of the people who own electric basses never really study the instrument seriously with a teacher. Yet, most bassists want to improve, and a large number buy method books and try to teach themselves. A typical high school student who has been playing bass may want to go to a music college. The first obstacle he or she confronts is that most colleges do not allow you to declare a major in *electric* bass. They often don't have an electric bass teacher, and because the instrument is so new (compared to the standard orchestral instruments), they haven't devised a curriculum. By this I mean that they don't have a program of various pieces that should be played at the many stages in your development.

There are some alternatives for getting into the school, even if you don't major in electric bass. One is to become a theory or composition major. Another is to take up the string bass, which has many things in common with the electric. However, the string bass world is quite different in terms of the types of music you would be expected to master on the college level. Funk, soul, and popping styles, for instance, are far removed from the typical college curriculum.

Many colleges offer something quite unique in the area of performance: the stage band. Such a band usually has from 14 to 20 people reading big band charts, and the bass parts present many challenges. There are notes written exactly as they are to be played, and there are also notes that must be interpreted—especially in jazz charts. Also, you will encounter chord symbols that will demand a lot of fast thinking in order for you to make up a good bass line on the spot. This is invaluable training for studio work.

Try to take as many theory and harmony classes as possible. It's not a bad idea to put off any composition, arranging, orchestration, and counterpoint classes until you have taken all the theory and harmony classes a school has to offer. When you have completed these requisites, you'll be better prepared to handle such advanced topics.

In the last few years, there have been a few open-minded schools that have opened their doors to the electric bassists. They have classes which may include from ten to 40 bassists in a single room. A lot of information is given out, but there is very little, if any, individual instruction. You're expected to motivate yourself to practice and you must remember all the details given out by the teacher.

Having taught in this class situation for four years, I feel qualified to say that very few players really can motivate themselves in a classroom situation. In my experience, I have found that the really talented and determined players will put in the time and effort to improve. The rest won't be able to motivate themselves as well.

However, in a private lesson situation the motivation is much stronger for all levels of bass players. You are paying for individualized attention, and for a period of an hour or so, you are getting help on a one-to-one basis. Problems relating to fingering, reading, theory, and technique are covered where they relate to you—on your particular level.

By Herb Mickman

Why You Should Learn To Read Music

Guitar Player **magazine March 1987**

It isn't such a terrible thing to be a musician who reads music. There seems to be a stigma surrounding a musician who is able to decipher those little notes and play them on his instrument. The standard joke in this area is when two musicians are chatting together: "Can you read music?" asks the first fellow. The second chap responds, "Not enough to hurt my playing." This erroneous attitude is a nasty obstacle in your musical path. To believe that anybody who can read a melodic line and interpret harmony and rhythms from a piece of paper will have their creative juices and improvisational skills hampered is silly. Reading music makes you free. It gives you a million opportunities to explore your bass in ways that you have never dreamed of before. If it weren't for my reading skills (thanks to a loving father who encouraged me to read as a young boy), I would never have been able to learn enough about music to play the way I do. My solos would not be as harmonically set-up as they are, and my rhythmic concepts and the music I compose would be drastically altered.

I will agree that there are plenty of world-class musicians who have made a name for themselves without being able to read a note. Not being able to read won't curtail your natural inquisitiveness. You will still have your enthusiasm to propel you into new sonic areas, and as a musician, you will grow. But the catch is, if you choose an area of music as your career choice, you'd better try like the dickens to succeed in that area, because if you don't make it as a non-reading musician, you have absolutely nothing to fall back on.

If you love your guitar or bass, there is no reason why you shouldn't put in an hour or two every day and learn to read. First of all, your career choices rapidly increase. Forgetting that I'm a soloist for one second, simply because I read, I'm hired by other artists as a sideman for their records. I play bass for TV shows and movies. I do jingles in the studios. I play with composers and jazz artists in live concerts, and I write out my own ideas to give to other musicians who can also read, which saves a lot of time. I teach, arrange music, and can play in almost any band with no rehearsal (except with Frank Zappa), do the gig, pocket the dough, and go home. All of this, *plus* doing my own bass videos, and pursuing many other musical possibilities—all because I read music.

I want you all to know that there are many opportunities for you in the music field. You can still try for rock stardom, jazz stardom, or any stardom you wish. Reading music gives you authenticity in your playing. It makes information instantly available, plus it puts music within your reach that you would have never thought of, or worse, never thought of practicing and playing. Reading music makes as much sense as reading English. Recently, there has been a lot of mention in the news about adult men and women in the U.S. who can't read a word of English. How limited these poor people must be! They can't read the directions on a medicine bottle, or know which exit to take off the freeway when driving out of town.

There are teachers in your community who can help you with your reading. They don't have to be bass teachers; piano teachers will do just fine. Work on Bach. His music is beautiful on an electric bass. Let your teachers give you some direction, and then, after you've practiced your lessons for the day, go to your garage with your buddies and turn up your amps. You *can* do both.

By Jeff Berlin

Some Books For Study

The following list of books for study includes methods and studies with material ranging from simple eighth-note rhythms to rock figures, syncopations, and some advanced exercises. Some will have to be ordered from the publisher if you can't find them in a music shop; many larger stores will be able to order them for you, so don't be afraid to ask. It would be a good idea to go through the first four books on the list before attempting the others.

Books 1, 2, and 5 are general methods, while 3 and 4 are straight eighth-note and sixteenth-note studies. Rock figures with a lot of syncopation are included in 5, 6, 12, 15, and 16. Books 7, 8, 10, 11, 13, and 14 are good for jazz reading.

1. *New Method For The Double Bass*, by F. Simandl [Carl Fischer, 62 Cooper Square, New York, NY 10003].
2. *Bob Haggart Bass Method* [Big Three Music, 729 Seventh Ave., New York, Ny 10019; and Robbins Music, 1350 Avenue Of The Americas, New York, NY 10019].
3. *First Book Of Practical Studies For Trombone, Book 1* and 2 [Belwin-Mills, 25 Deshon Dr., Melville, NY 11747].
4. *Fun With The Trombone* and *More Fun With The Trombone* [Mel Bay, Pacific, MO 63069].
5. *How To Play The Electric Bass* [Warner Bros., 75 Rockefeller, New York, NY 10019].
6. *Electric Bass Lines, Volume 1, 2, 3, 4,* and 5, by Carol Kaye [Gwyn Publ., Box 5900, Sherman Oaks, CA 91413].
7. *Rhythms Complete* (bass clef edition) [Chas. Colin, 315 W. 53rd St., New York, NY 10019].
8. *30 Studies In Swing* (bass clef edition) [Sam Fox Music, 1841 Broadway, New York, NY 10023].
9. *Streamlined Etudes For Trombone* [Sam Fox Music].
10. *Ray Brown Bass Method* [Ray Brown Music, Box 270, Hollywood Station, Hollywood, CA 90028].
11. *Dance Band Reading And Interpretations* (bass clef edition) [Sam Fox Music].
12. *Basic Electric Bass, Volume 1, 2, 3, 4,* and 5 [Sam Fox Music].
13. *Jazz Improvisations For Bass Clef Instruments* [Gwyn Publ.].
14. *The Evolving Bassist,* by Rufus Reid [Myriad, Ltd., Lock Box 503, 2138 E. 75th St., Chicago, IL. 60649].
15. *Rhythmic Figures For Bassists, Volume 1* (eighth-notes) and *Volume 2* (sixteenth-notes) [Charles Hansen, 1860 West Ave., Miami Beach FL 33139].
16. *Electric Bass, Books 1, 2, and 3,* by Dan Dean (bass clef & TAB, record) Hal Leonard, 8112 W. Bluemound Rd., Milwaukee, WI 53213.
17. *The Studio Bassist, Books 1, 2, and 3* by Dan Dean (bass clef & TAB, record) Hal Leonard.

Chapter 2:
Reading

Reading

Guitar Player **magazine   October 1974**

Reading In The Bass Clef

Most professionals take sightreading for granted—yours truly is no exception. However, through teaching, one becomes aware of the reading problems that students experience needlessly. I learned to read under pressure in studio work and although it was tough, there were many "shortcuts" I learned that can be passed on to you to make reading fun and easy.

To familiarize yourself with fundamentals in notes and timing, a book is necessary to refer to, such as *Easy Electric Bass* (from the Gwyn Publishing Co.). Fundamentals, such as quarter-notes, names of notes, where they are on the instrument, ties, dots, flats, sharps, naturals, and key signatures, should be practiced from one of the many books on the market. One problem that arises when you start this learning process is to keep boredom from striking. Boredom precedes a state of mind that stops one from learning, thereby causing the student to think it is very difficult to learn to sightread.

If you learn a few notes on the bass, you can find other notes around them by relating back to the known notes. If the second note looks higher than the first, it is higher in pitch, and so on for lower notes (lower pitch).

One should get into the habit of writing beat lines (to pat your foot on) rather than writing in all the intricate 1-e-an-a garbage—studio musicians do this to aid reading. (See Figure 1.) In 4/4 time, any note with a down-beat marking is played when your foot pats down—any other note is played when your foot is in the air—as simple as that. You aim for the downbeats. Intricate meter (timing) patterns should be memorized—like learning the times tables. Sixteenth-note patterns are figured out in double time (8/8), where instead of four beats to each bar (4/4 time), you play as if there are eight beats to the bar. (See Figure 2.) Any pattern that has double beams (sixteenth-notes) indicates a double-time (8/8) feel and should be felt in that time.

To go about finding notes on the bass, a little knowledge of the basic scale is necessary. At first, I actually wrote some of the names of notes above the staff to assist me. However, you really start learning more by reading "fun" patterns and relating one note to another. *Scales tend to inhibit your creative ear.*

By writing downbeats to your music, you involve yourself immediately with the "feel" of meter—coordinating your foot and eyes with the music. If you write in the mechanical countings (1-e-an-a, etc.), you might get stuck reading those and not looking at the notes, hence the need for beat markings which the eye can catch without detracting from the actual notes.

Other tricks of reading involve scanning over the notes to aim for the downbeats which are used for reference purposes in meter. When music is copied or engraved, it is usually mathematically spaced so the eye can follow the logical downbeats of the notes. You can usually find the downbeats in the way eighth- and sixteenth-notes are lumped together by a common beam. Usually the first note of the connecting beam is the downbeat:

The only exception is when a rest comes first, such as:

It has been stated before that sixteenth-notes indicate an 8/8 (doubletime) feel. Meter (timing of notes) is either in 2 or 3 (each beat divisible by 2 or 3) in all music (see Figure 4). The only time music is written incorrectly is usually in 3, meaning triplets. That is, when you see dotted eighths and sixteenths mixed in with triplets, the music is played in triplet form (in 3) but written wrong to make it easier to read. For example:

incorrect   same as   correct

As you learn to read notes, several guides may come to you such as: visual recognition of octaves, learning the bottom, middle, and top staff line notes, ledger line notes, commonly used notes (C, F, G, A, etc.) as well as relative notes (C to D, A to G, etc.). Try to avoid tricks such as F-A-C-E spells FACE—this has no meaning to music and deters you from actual reading, much like marking (1-e-an-a) to meter rather than feeling the beat.

It is not essential to know how to sightread to play good music. A good ear is important for learning bass lines from records and following chords to new tunes. But, if you would like to be a well-rounded musician and be able to have doors opened for you, whether it be for fun or money, you must be able to read. Attitude is very important. If you find yourself getting bored or forcing yourself to practice when a mental block comes, this negative feeling is going to keep you from the fun of discovering the little tricks of reading. Take a break, come back later and study, and make sure you have absolute quiet. *Be sure to keep your eyes on the music.* Even though you will memorize a short pattern very quickly, you learn to read by way of "osmosis," for familiar patterns will be recognized in new situations and you will be reading in a short time. This is the quickest, easiest and best way to learn how to sightread.

Attempt to write down any unique bass line you hear on a record that you particularly like. By writing you also learn to read. Every chance you get to read arrangements, go jump in the pool and do it. It's surprising what you can learn under pressure.

By Carol Kaye

Figure 1.   **(Arrows indicate pitch direction)**

Figure 2.   **(feet in 8/8 time)**

1 and 2 and   3 and 4   and   1   2   3   4

Figure 3.   **(feet in 8/8 time)**

Figure 4.   **(in 2)**   **(in 3)**

Using Interval Relationships For Transposing

Guitar Player **magazine** **November 1978**

One of the first things you learn in a harmony class is that each note in a major scale is given a Roman numeral to designate its function (see Figure 5). Distances between scale notes are called *intervals*. The smallest interval in traditional music is a half-step, or semitone. It is the distance from one fret to the adjacent one. You can see that no other note could be placed between the two (see Figure 6). A two-fret interval is called a whole-step, or whole-tone (see Figure 7). There is a definite construction pattern for major scales: All the intervals between consecutive scale notes are whole-tones, except the III-IV and VII-VIII intervals, which are half-steps (see Figure 5).

Figure 5.

C major scale   half-step   half-step

I   II   III   IV   V   VI   VII   VIII

Key To Notational Symbols

The following symbols are used in *Electric Bass Guitar* to indicate fingerings, techniques, and effects commonly used in bass guitar music notation.

4● : Left-hand fingering is designated by small Arabic numerals near note heads (1 = first finger, 2 = second finger, 3 = third finger, 4 = little finger; and T = thumb).

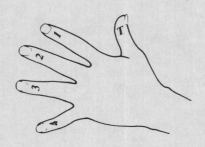

p● : Right-hand fingering is designated by letters (*p* = thumb, *i* = index, *m* = middle, *a* = ring, and *l* = little).

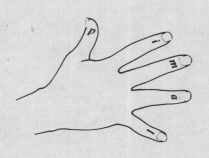

②● : A circled number (1-6) indicates the string on which a particular note is to be played.

⊓ : Pick downstroke.

V : Pick upstroke.

C V : The C indicates a full barre; the Roman numeral designates the proper fret.

¢ V : The C indicates a first finger half-barre covering either the first three or four strings, depending on what is called for in the notation.

₃ 🖐 : Partial barre with the designated finger.

〰 : Left-hand finger vibrato.

₇ ⁽B⁾ : Bend; play the first note and bend to the required pitch (bent note is in parentheses). See tab explanation.

⁽B⁾ ₇ : Reverse bend; strike an already bent note, then allow it to return to its unbent pitch (bent note is in parentheses).

₇ ⁽H⁾ ₉ : Hammer-on (lower note to higher).

₉ ⁽P⁾ ₇ : Pull-off (higher note to lower).

Ⓣ : Indicates right-hand tapping technique.

3⁄5ˢ : Slide; play first note and slide to the next pitch (in tab, an upward slide is indicated with an upward-slanting line, while a downward slide is indicated with a downward-slanting line).

↕ : Strum (an arrowhead is often used to indicate direction).

ᵣₐˢ ↕ : Rasgueado.

//// : Indicates desired rhythm for chordal accompaniment. (The choice of voicings is up to the player.)

How Tablature Works. The horizontal lines represent the bass guitar's strings, the top line standing for the high G. The numbers designate the frets to be played. For instance, a 2 positioned on the first line would mean to play the 2nd fret on the first string (0 indicates an open string). Time values are indicated on the coinciding lines of standard notation seen directly above the tablature. Read tablature from left to right in the conventional manner.

Chord Diagrams. In all chord diagrams, vertical lines represent the strings, and horizontal lines represent the frets. The following symbols are used:

——— : Nut; indicates first position.

x : Muted string, or string not played.

o : Open string.

⌢ : Barre (partial or full).

● : Placement of left-hand fingers.

III : Roman numerals indicate the fret at which a chord is located.

1 : Arabic numerals indicate left-hand fingering, (e.g., 1 = index, etc.).

Figure 6.

half-step intervals

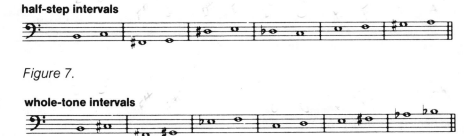

Figure 7.

whole-tone intervals

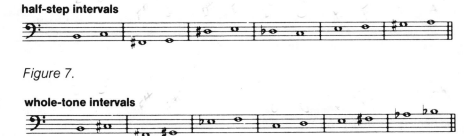

If you have to transpose a song from the key in which it is written to another, it is a lot easier if you use the numeral names for each note. For example, if you had a chord progression in *F*, where *F* went to *D*, you should think of it as I going to VI. If you had to move the song to the key of *E*♭, the chords would be *E*♭ and *C* (I and VI in the key of *E*♭). In *D*, the I and VI would be *D* and *B*, respectively. Needless to say, the better you know the scales, the better you will be able to transpose. In Nashville, for instance, many of the record dates have written parts that consist only of numeral names.

The following exercises deal with the diatonic 3rds (see Figure 8), which are adjacent 3rds within a scale. Sections C and D should be fingered with all three notes of each triplet in one position (so that you don't have to move your hand up or down the neck in the middle of the figure). Play these in all keys, starting in the lowest positions and using the open strings to avoid unnecessary shifting. These exercises are excellent for improving your ear, knowledge of keys, and fingering patterns.

By Herb Mickman

Figure 8.

Diatonic thirds (C major scale)

Repeat Signs In Charts

Guitar Player **magazine August 1986**

It's amazing that there is not a whole lot of repeat notation in method books. But I've learned some useful information about the world of repeat markings, how they work, and how you can make sight reading easier.

Figure 9 shows a measure that repeats in the second bar. This is often written with a repeat sign, as in the second bar of Figure 10. In Figure 11, we see another way of indicating a repeat, using a sign at the end of the bar (the double line with the double dots). In Figure 12, we see bars 2, 3, and 4 with repeat markings—to indicate repeating the first bar three times. Figure 13 tells us the same thing by having the number over the second bar. In this case, it means to repeat the first bar three times.

Figure 14 shows a two-bar phrase followed by a repeat sign that indicates a duplication of the first two bars. Figure 15 is a bar with four dots at its end; this means that the bar repeats more than once, and the "6x" means to play it six times. For Figure 16, we play the first two bars, and then go into the first ending; then we encounter a repeat sign (a double line and dots), meaning to go back and play the first two bars followed by the second ending. The word *fine* indicates the end of the piece (this word isn't always included). Figure 17 has the same first and second ending, and after playing them, you go back to the beginning again, and you finally take the third ending.

Figure 18 has us playing the first four bars until we see *D.C. al coda* (D.C. is short for *Da Capo*); this means to go back to the beginning and continue until you see a *coda* sign (it's shown here at the end of the second bar). At that point, you do not go to the third bar; instead, you go to the coda, which has that same sign (and the word "coda" after it).

In Figure 19, we play the first eight bars, and then we see a sign called a *Del Segno al coda* (Del Segno is abbreviated *D.S.*). It means to go back to the Del Segno sign (bar 5) from that point, and play until you see a coda sign (bar 7). After you have reached the coda, play through to the end.

In our final example, Figure 20, play the first four bars and proceed to the first ending. Then go back to the beginning and take the second ending. Play until you come to the *D.S. al fine* sign. It means that you should go directly to the *D.S.* sign (second bar of the second ending) and play until the *fine* ending. (If you're wondering about the symbol that looks like an "I" turned on its side with a number 4 above it, it means four bars of rest.)

Hopefully these examples will wipe away a few musical cobwebs for you. As you read more and more charts, you'll notice that many arrangers and copyists have their own musical shorthand.

By Herb Mickman

Tricks Of The Score

Many arrangers have their own personal notational symbols, so it's impossible to cover all the various musical directions that can be indicated. However, there are a lot of important things that are hardly ever included in bass method books.

Figure 21 is a two-bar section with slashes to indicate the beats. Each slash gets one beat, so bar 1 is four quarter-notes. Bar 2 is two beats of Abm7 and two beats of Db7. A good rule is to try getting the root of each chord on the frist beat in which it occurs. Also, I recommend using mostly chordal notes in your bass lines until you get more experience.

In Figure 22 we have two bars without the slashes. This is the same idea as Figure 21. If two different chords come up in a bar, we assume they fall on beats 1 and 3 (see the second bar). In Figure 23 we have some chords fall on the fourth beat of the bar. Be sure to play the chord's root on the fourth beat. Figure 24 does not have a chord symbol, but instead has a quarter-note and then three slashes. The intention is to repeat the first note three more times.

Figure 25 is a 3/4 part with a variety of rhythmic figures indicated by various symbols. Notice that the flags and dots attached to notes correspond with the same indications in standard notation. Figure 26 has horizontal lines through the stems of some of the notes. One line means to divide the quarter-note into two eighth-notes. A double line means to play sixteenth-notes. Figure 27 tells you to play a D7 for four bars. In Figure 28 you really have to think fast to place certain bass notes on the strong beats. Figure 29 is a typical notation for jazz choruses; the "32" means that the song is 32 bars, and you'll have to find the chord changes further back in the chart. The order of the soloists is tenor sax, trumpet, and then piano. At the end of the piano solo, you resume reading the chart.

Figure 30 is a typical ending in the bass world. It's got a few special symbols to get the composer's desired phrasing. The dot over a note means to play it short (detached). The line indicates giving that note its full value (not short). In bar 2 we have a slur line over the eighth-notes, which means to play them *legato* (smoothly connected). Also remember how to articulate eighth-notes in jazz phrasing—like an eighth-note triplet with the first two notes tied.

A few important points: Concentrate on keeping good time and keeping your place in the chart, no matter what. If you see something coming up that you can't play, just play however much of it that you can, and keep going. It's important to learn to read two or more bars ahead. This takes practice, so read at home using a metronome to develop more accuracy with a variety of rhythmic figures.

By Herb Mickman

Guitar Player **magazine September 1986**

Figure 21.

Figure 22.

Figure 23.

Figure 24.

Figure 25.

Figure 26.

Figure 27.

Figure 28.

Figure 29.   Figure 30.

Robert Townsend And His Partners In Crime TV Show. We now take you live to the recording of the HBO Television Special *Robert Townsend And His Partners In Crime.* The call is for 3:30 P.M., Saturday, December 19, 1987, at the Henry Fonda Theatre in Hollywood. Patrice Rushen is musical director, arranger, and conductor, and the show (a comedy special) will be taped live at 7:00 P.M. and aired simultaneously for nationwide TV.

Patrice wrote the music for the play-ons and play-offs, and they'll give you a glimpse of what you might have to sight-read if you do a job of this nature. Most of the challenge is being ready to play as soon as one of the performers is introduced. Then you must pay attention to the act; as soon as it's finished, listen for a two-beat count from Patrice for the playoff. It goes by pretty fast, so the best advice in this situation is to be prepared, have your instrument in good working order, make sure you're in tune, use good cables, etc. You don't want to encounter any technical problems! The rest is just being alert and playing with confidence.

Note that play-ons and play-offs 1 and 3 should be transposed down an octave.

By Jeff Berlin and Nathan East

"Play-On/Play-Off Music"   ## By Patrice Rushen

Overcoming Poorly-Written Bass Charts

***Guitar Player* magazine November 1978**

Once I played a big band rehearsal and ran into half a dozen things in the bass parts that made the charts difficult to read. I've been seeing these same six things now for the past 22 years, and I wish we could make arrangers and copyists aware of them. Some of these "rocks" are encountered by other instrumentalists as well, while others are found only on bass parts. I've listed some of these stumbling blocks, and I have tried to show a better way to notate them.

In Figure 31 the notes are written out of the range of the bass (you'll have to transpose up an octave). A rhythmic figure with chord symbols is shown in Figure 32. This is typical guitar notation, but for bass players it would be easier to have the actual notes written out.

Figure 33 shows how some arrangers write a rhythm in such a way that you cannot easily see the third beat of the bar. The rhythm shown in Figure 32 is similar, though it is much more common. You have to be a mathematician to sight-read (Figure 33).

Figure 34 illustrates the symptoms of what I call "poor copyist's bass line." The arranger told the copyist to write a walking bass line, and the copyist was just not familiar with bass line construction. Notice the correction which has its roots on the strong beats. Sometimes a tune gets recorded with wrong notes inserted by a copyist, and the bass player gets the blame. Figure 35 demonstrates a pet peeve of mine: The incomplete chord symbols just don't give you a chance to sound your best—especially on a solo. Some people write only the root name. How are you going to choose the other notes when you don't know if the chord is major, or minor, or whatever? Just giving the root isn't enough. Figure 36 is a typical bass figure, but without phrasing markings. Only an experienced player would play it with the right conception the first time through. Because it says "slow swing," the quarter-notes are short and the eighth-notes are played legato, with a triplet feel.

By Herb Mickman

Figure 31.

Figure 32.

Figure 33.

Figure 34.

Figure 35.

Figure 36.

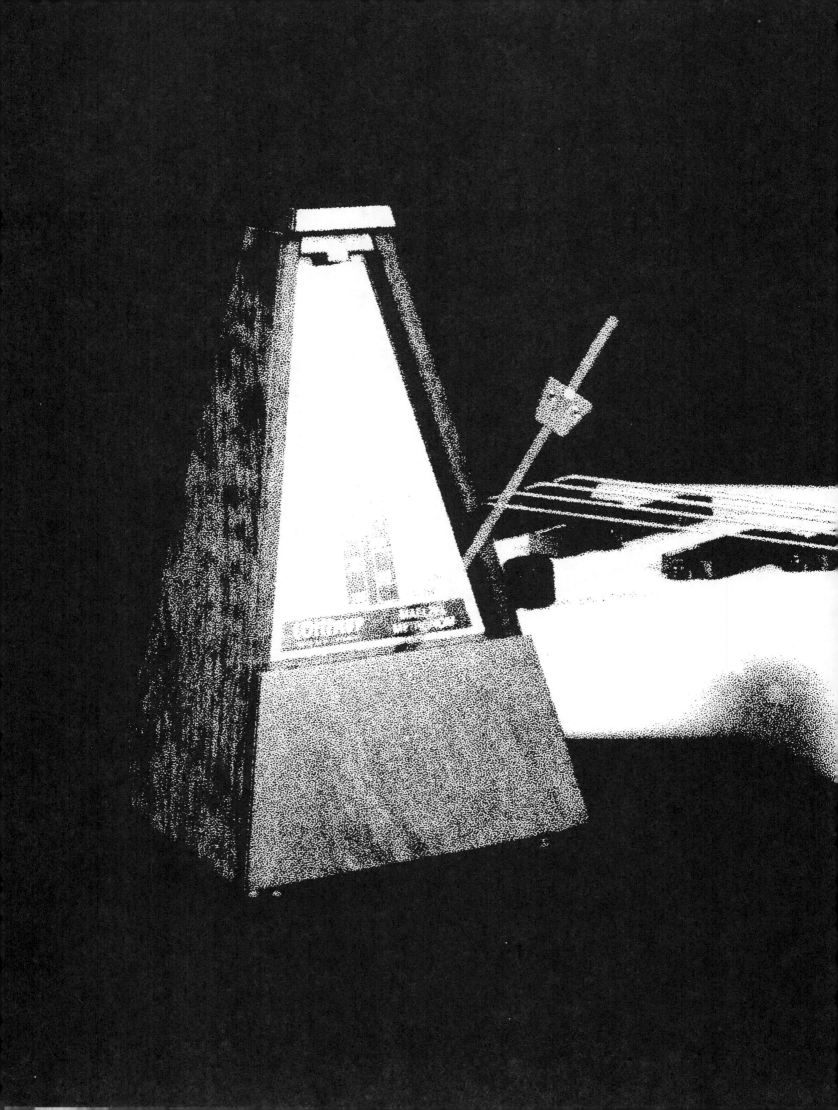

Chapter 3:
Practicing

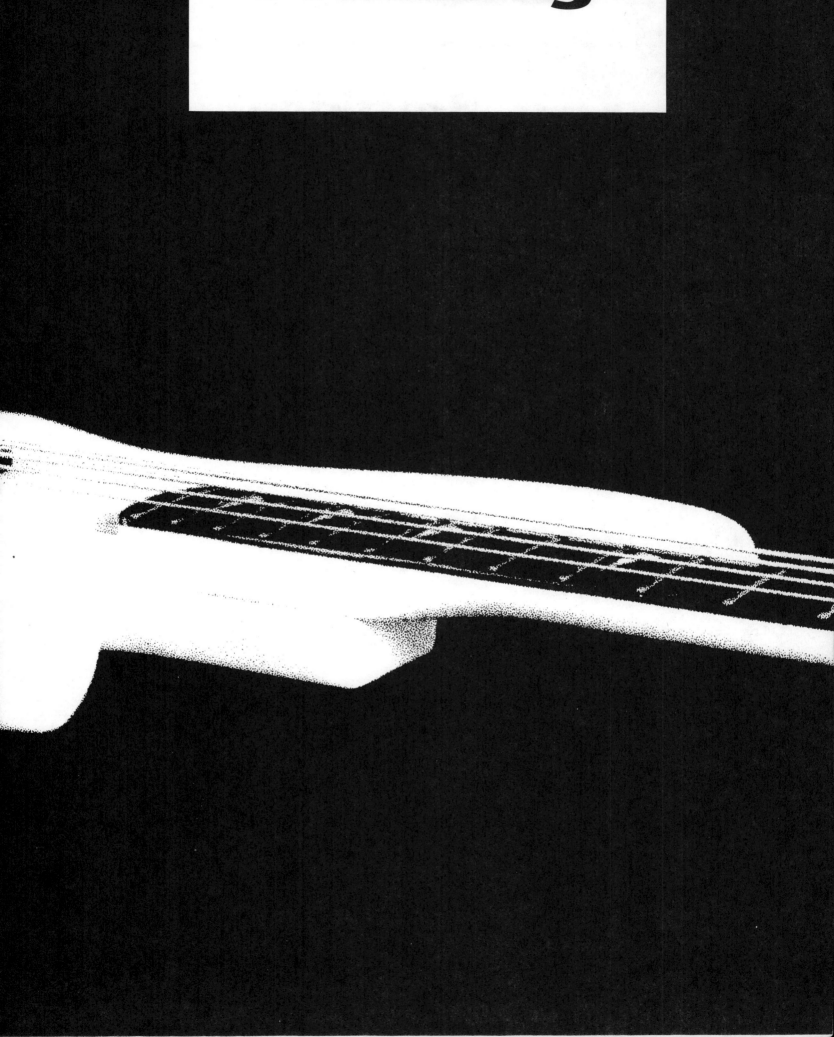

Practicing

Target Practice

Guitar Player magazine May, June 1981

Back in 1957, I was living in New York City, and I was fortunate enough to study string bass with the late Fred Zimmermann. He was the first-chair bassist in the New York Philharmonic Orchestra for over 30 years and probably the most famous bass teacher in the country. His former students were in symphony orchestras in many nations, and bass players came from all over the world to study with him. His most prominent student in the jazz idiom was Eddie Gomez, although many other well-known bassists studied with him, including Paul Chambers, Charles Mingus, and Red Mitchell.

One of my problems was quite common among beginning musicians—playing in tune. Mr. Z had a very helpful routine called "target practice." In the following target practice exercises, play all the notes on the G string, starting in the lowest position on the bass: 1/2-position (you may know it as the first fret).

Work on these exercises every day. Each measure should be played over and over many times until the notes connect smoothly, without buzzes or sliding noises. On a fretless bass, you must be much more concerned with exact intonation.

The first two lines of the exercise are easy, but later sections have bigger intervals and will require you to play slower to feel the shifts. Always shift from one position to another without looking at your left hand.

Mr. Zimmermann probably never held an electric bass in his hands, but I'm sure he would be glad to know his target practice is being passed on.

By Herb Mickman

Progressive Exercises

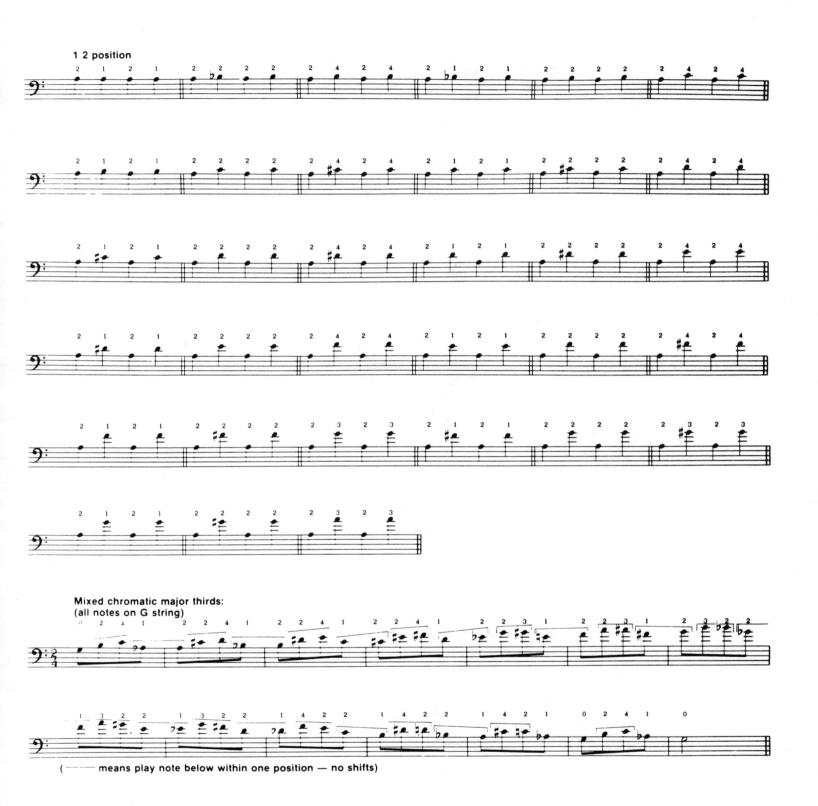

1 2 position

Mixed chromatic major thirds:
(all notes on G string)

(——— means play note below within one position — no shifts)

Practicing With The Metronome

Shortly after my first few music lessons, my parents were told that using a metronome would help to improve my sense of rhythm. The metronome I got was an old-style wind-up model with the pendulum that swayed back and forth. I found it very difficult to play with at the tender age of eight.

Guitar Player **magazine September 1982**

Not long after I got the metronome, I dropped it, and it broke. I didn't use one again until ten years later. I had a drummer friend who used to practice with one while playing on a drum pad, and he said, "If you can hear the metronome while you are playing quarter-notes, you are off." He asked me to try playing quarter-notes evenly with the metronome, and I didn't do as well as I thought I would. It was then that I saw the benefits that could be derived from practicing with a metronome. So, the next day I went to the neighborhood music store and bought an electric metronome.

It really helped settle my sense of time. When I began working with the metronome, I would set it to click once for every quarter-note in a 4/4 setting. I would then write down the metronome tempos on the page I worked on each day, so that I knew what my limitations were. Then, each subsequent day I would start at the last tempo that was comfortable, and try to surpass it—just a notch or two.

Soon I became aware that I didn't need the metronome ticking on all four beats. So I had it tick on beats 1 and 3. A tempo of 120 then became a tempo of 60, etc. A few weeks later a trumpet player told me to set the metronome to click on beats 2 and 4 for a 4/4 measure. He said that it would swing better.

At first, I wasn't comfortable, but after a while I noticed that this way I got better feeling—especially for jazz and improvising. When the metronome was set to click on the first and third beats, it felt stiff in comparison to its setting on second and fourth.

I also began to practice not only etudes, but also jazz melodies with the metronome. I put the most comfortable tempo number on the page, and I always strived to increase that tempo until it was at the same speed as the record. However, there are certain things that a bass will never get out as quickly as a saxophone, trumpet, or piano. I soon learned to accept what could be done and be happy with it.

Below are some patterns I have made up from the familiar C major scale. They should be practiced with the metronome at a comfortable tempo, where there is no struggling and no wrong notes. You should be able to play the exercises evenly in tempo. After working with each one and noting the metronome's tempo marking, play the exercises in all 12 keys. Do not advance to another exercise until you can play the first one in all keys smoothly. Don't expect to double your tempo in an afternoon. Start with the one-octave scales, and eventually try the two-octave ones. Play Figure 1 and Figure 2 both ascending and descending. Also, after playing Figure 4 with the patterns indicated (one eighth-note and two sixteenth-notes), reverse the pattern (two sixteenth-notes followed by an eighth-note). Do the same for Figure 6.

Figure 1.

Figure 2.

Figure 3.

Figure 4.

Figure 5.

Figure 6.

Figure 7.

Bass players today are expected to have a great feel for time in many types of rhythmic grooves that didn't exist, say, ten years ago, and sight-reading has become far more complex. One of the keys to becoming a great sight-reader is to have the sounds of many common rhythms memorized. This ingraining of patterns comes from playing particular rhythms many times at all kinds of tempos. The first step often is working through the rhythm slowly, while the metronome keeps time for you.

In Figure 8 are some great off-beats to be practiced. Try to play each measure at least four times perfectly before moving to the next one. Determine which tempo provided by the metronome is most comfortable for you, and write it down. Try to increase your speed., and keep track of your progress.

Figure 9 has four rhythmic variations on the C major scale. Play each pattern up and down one octave in all 12 keys before going to the next one. Eventually work them up to two octaves. Once you master these, you can apply the same ideas to minor and modal scales.

Figure 10 deals with some scale sequences containing various rhythmic displacements. Play the first one (A) slowly until you hear what is going on in the rhythm. Once you

Figure 8.

Figure 9.

Figure 10.

can play it perfectly in *C*, try it in the other keys over one octave. Spend a good week on mastering them. The second part (B) contains diatonic third intervals (occurring naturally within the scale) that follow similar rhythmic schemes.

You will have to determine which tempos are best for you simply by checking your ability to produce strong, even rhythms as well as correctly intonated notes. This type of practice is like weightlifting: If you lay off for a while, you'll have to adjust the metronome's setting back a notch or two and work back up to the tempo you had achieved.

By Herb Mickman

Making The Most Of A Rehearsal

Guitar Player **magazine August 1988**

There is a communal event that takes place behind closed doors, one that can establish musical ties and personal friendships between colleagues, or utterly decimate a band and precipitate personal hatred and plans for revenge among fellow musicians for years to come. I am talking about *rehearsal*.

This article is being written in Paris, France, where I'm playing in a trio with John McLaughlin and drummer/percussionist Trilok Gurtu. For the next 12 weeks we'll be touring all over Europe; in August we'll be in the United States playing with Miles Davis and/or Chick Corea.

Our entire touring itinerary can only exist because of one very important element that can make or break any group performing in front of an audience who bought their tickets in order to be blown away by the musicians—or to damn them all to hell if they fail to do so! The glue holding it all together is *practice*.

We've based our immediate musical future and ability to earn a living as professional players on a two-week investment. In these two weeks, we came up with the new music, set it to memory, updated the songs daily, practiced enough to integrate the music into our bodies (instead of calculated run-throughs, which is the way all new music is approached), established our time relationships (or groove interplay), learned which is the best way to relate as live interacting musicians, found the best order for the tunes, and learned how to relate as people—respecting each other's way of being individuals—in a close living and working relationship.

Let's forget about chops and licks and all that goofy technique stuff for a minute. Here's how ro rehearse with purpose and really accomplish something. First, you only get out what you put into your rehearsals. How many rehearsals have you attended in which you stop every ten minutes for a cigarette break, or somebody runs down to the deli for Cokes and sandwiches, or you hang out and shoot the breeze while playing a tune every now and then? Is that rehearsing? No way, Jose! A rehearsal is supposed to be a time of work. *Hard* work. This hard work ethic shouldn't be a problem, though, because it's supposed to be *fun* to play an instrument and learn new music, right? That's how you get better. If you practiced for, let's say, two hours and then you took a break, you'd be putting concentrated time into your band and your instrument. With McLaughlin, we practiced up to nine hours every day and took some time for lunch and dinner. We worked until we were exhausted, but we knew we earned something from it. Pick your own time schedule, and *earn* something musical for your band and yourself.

Second, have some music prepared before the rehearsal. A lot of bands get together and mess around until something emerges. This is often a good method of developing a group sound, but it doesn't *always* work out that way. It's hard to accomplish anything when everyone is simultaneously playing something that has little to do with each other's music. If you have at least a form, some chords, or a melody prepared in advance, you're in a better situation to develop a song. The Beatles did this. There's a tape of a Beatles rehearsal where Paul McCartney is teaching "Let It Be" to the band. He played piano and sang a rough outline of it, with the chord names replacing some of the words, just so that the others could get the changes in their heads.

Get the picture? Even if you've prepared a small sketch of something, it is a big head start for your band. Look at some of Yes' earlier albums. If you look at the writing credit for the tune "Close To The Edge," you will see that the listed composer is Jon Anderson. Certainly he didn't come in with every part arranged, but rather with a good sketch. The band picked up on it and collectively developed a masterpiece of modern rock. They practiced for hours, as well, and created a band sound that is still appreciated today, even in light of their more phenomenal recent album successes.

By Jeff Berlin

Flexibility And Breaking Old Habits

Guitar Player **magazine   April 1977**

Years ago I found that after playing the same bass parts over and over again, I would tend to form habits that later would create problems when I tried to do something different. Suppose for five years I'd been playing a *C* scale using the fingering 2, open, 1, 2, open, 1, 2, 3, and then someone gave me music (or I wrote music) requiring me to play a *C* scale using a different fingering, because of the way the scale was placed in the particular song or passage. I would have to break that old habit of fingering the scale and play it another way for the new passage.

Now, a way to rid yourself of at least 70 percent of these sorts of problems is to : 1) become very familiar with the fingerboard and know where all of the notes are; and 2) make your hand flexible enough to be able to play all over the neck by taking something as simple as a *C* scale and playing it three or four different ways on the instrument.

I can remember many times when I played music written by Chick Corea, some of the lines he'd write would, at first, seem technically unfamiliar to me, possibly because when he wrote them he was sitting down at a keyboard instrument. I have found that keyboard bass lines require quite unorthodox techniques when they are played on an electric bass. Personally, I find this very rewarding, because by playing these sorts of things I learn something that I might not have discovered on my own.

When I was in college, I auditioned for the double bass section of the Philadelphia Orchestra. One of the things I was preparing was a book of exercises which actually were excerpts of music composed by Richard Strauss. Boy, let me tell you—Richard Strauss wrote some of the most difficult stuff for bass I've ever played! He had no mercy!

Here's a piece of music I wrote for guitar and bass which should help bassists develop flexibility. Both instruments fluctuate back and forth between *A* and *B* ♭maj. Practice this duet at a very slow tempo, and gradually increase your speed until you can play it in a fast cut time.

By Stanley Clarke

"Duet For Bass And Guitar"   **By Stanley Clarke**

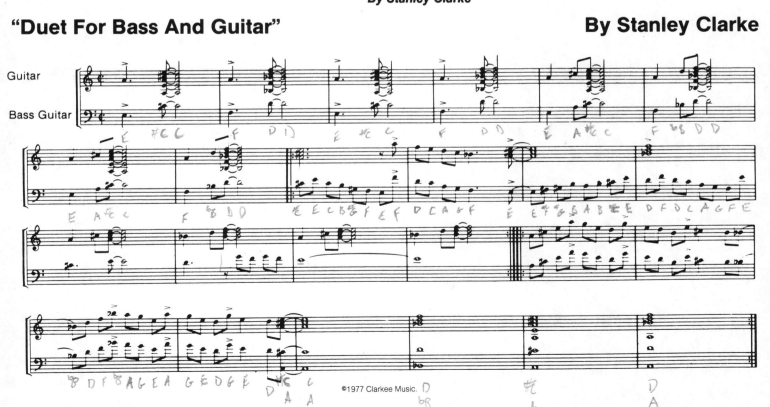

Chapter 4:
Technique

Technique

Synchronizing Your Hands

Guitar Player magazine October 1987

Warming up is a vital component of any performance, regardless of the instrument being played. For electric bassists, developing an effective warm-up routine is a technique in itself. Although the following warm-ups will loosen the fingers, they don't sound like your typical exercises; they actually have more of a bass-line quality. Practicing is much more fun when it improves your chops, and also sounds like music. I always try to kill two birds with one stone.

Figure 1 is a good way to wake up the right-hand fingers. Start at a comfortable tempo, and try to make it as even as possible, alternating between the first and second fingers. Try to play each note with the same dynamics as the note before it. One of the reasons I like this exercise so much is because it reminds me of the bass line in the song "What Is Hip" by Tower Of Power [*Live And In Living Color*, Warner Bros., BS 2924]. It's over a decade old, but it's still, in my opinoin, one of the most brilliant bass lines of all time (thanks, Francis Rocco Prestia). The natural finger to start this exercise with is the right-hand index finger to see if you feel any difference. This will help balance the right-hand fingerings.

Figure 2 coordinates both the left and right hands. This sixteenth-note exercise is fun to work up to a fast tempo. Of course, remember to play each note evenly and with the same dynamics. Although the faster tempo sounds more impressive, this is one of those exercises that is equally important to learn slowly. Certain characteristics of this exercise remind me of a Weather Report-type bass line as played by the late Jaco Pastorius.

Learn to play Figure 3 slowly, too, and speed it up as it feels more comfortable. This exercise is good target-shooting in jumping strings with the right-hand fingers. Play it using the high *E* on the *G* string and the low *E* on the *A* string.

Figure 4 is good for stretching the left-hand fingers. Just repeat the pattern on the first bar in half-steps all the way up and down the neck.

Again, these exercises are intended to sound musical, as well as build up your fingers. Five to ten minutes apiece is a good time to spend on them each day. Then see if you can invent some new ones.

By Nathan East

Figure 1.

Figure 2.

Figure 3.

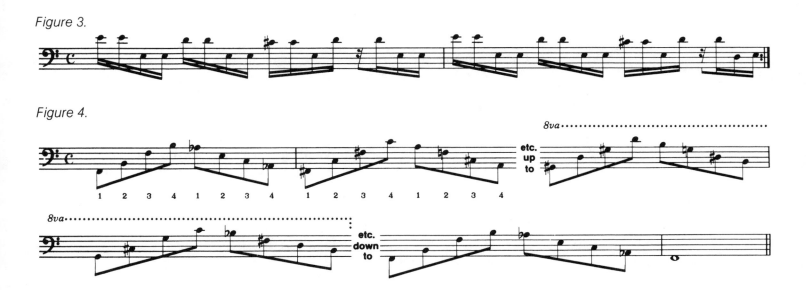

Figure 4.

Bass Popping Technique

Guitar Player magazine February 1980

Without a doubt, one of the most popular sounds produced by today's bassists is the "pop," or "slap"—a piercing, snappy effect that moves the bass line to the foreground of even the most lavishly orchestrated music. Most often heard in a funk context, the popping of notes is becoming increasingly diversified to the point of being firmly planted in numerous popular musical settings. Although popped notes show up frequently (listen to the radio, TV, or records—they're everywhere), many bassists have either avoided the style or failed to master the technique. Surprisingly, for as good as it sounds, getting the snap is not really difficult. With a solid start and a bit of practice, any bass player can assimilate popping, and make it another natural part of his or her style. Try it—you may even surprise yourself and bring out a facet of your playing that you never knew was waiting to be freed.

Even though numerous well-known bass guitarists incorporate this technique, nobody knows for sure the musician who first popped a string. When the string bass initially became popular in familiar forms of music in the early part of this century, some players actually hit the strings with a drumstick to get a crisper attack and more volume. Some literally flogged their strings with the right hand—a similar approach, but naturally one that required a good, strong hand.

Such techniques never really translated to the electric bass since players were generally pleased with their equipment's volume. But in the 1960s, a time of rapidly increasing volume and experimentation, new approaches were tried. Credit for bringing the popping technique to popular music is generally given to Larry Graham, who played bass with Sly & The Family Stone and later Graham Central Station. It was the culmination of his early experiences in a drummerless duo with his mother that led him to a more percussive style. From the first pops and snaps of his teens Graham built a technique that became one of the most identifiable features of Sly's music.

In the 1970s other bassists emerged with this popping technique in their bags of tricks. Among them were Stanley Clarke, Louis Johnson, Verdine White of Earth, Wind & Fire, and the late Jaco Pastorius of Weather Report. In almost every form of popular music today, there is at least one outstanding popper.

I first learned bass popping a few years ago from my old friend, Stanley Clarke, who had replaced me in pianist Horace Silver's band in 1970 when I left to join Mongo Santamaria. While on vacation in Florida, I met Stanley again, and I asked him to show me how to "play that thing with your thumb." The basics Stanley taught me were the key. The rest only required practice.

An important consideration for bass players wishing to learn this style is proper strings. Often the strings in a particular set are not balanced with respect to sound output and flexibility. You can generally deal with the uneven volume levels by raising or lowering the pickup's pole pieces, or adjusting the height of the pickup itself. But obtaining strings with consistent suppleness may pose a problem.

You want strings that give when you pull them, and spring back after you pluck them. Try the various brands, ask music dealers what they recommend, and ask fellow bass players what they've found in their travels. For the brightest tone, check out round-wound, half-round, or quarter-round strings. Flatwounds will most often lack the bite that the other varieties have. Also, remember that a string's flexibility may not be related to its gauge. Variables such as the materials used in construction, the length of your bass, and the string gauge's relationship to its open pitch may all affect performance.

Posture also enters into popping. Make sure that you place your hands in a comfortable position. There are two basic ways to place the right arm and hand to facilitate the technique. In Figures 5 and 6, note how the right arm lies comfortably on the body of the instrument. The thumb can either be in an upward position—parallel to the strings (Figure 5)—or lie perpendicular to the strings (Figure 6). In both cases, notice how the first and second fingers on the right hand are poised directly over the G and D strings. By having them in such close proximity to the strings, it is easy to snap or pluck them on an upstroke, while the thumb can hit on the downstroke.

Figure 5.

Figure 6.

These three exercises are designed to help you gain control over your thumb. They should be played on the E and A strings. Although they're not very complicated, they should be played with care nonetheless. Count each beat evenly (or use a metronome), and try to attack each note cleanly, so that the sound is crisp, not mushy. Note that the letter "T" above the note means to hit it with the thumb.

Exercise 1.   *Exercise 2.*

Exercise 3.

Since your first and second fingers are placed right over the G and D strings, they are always ready to snap; you may snap either string with either finger. Do this closer to the fingerboard than to the bridge, since there is less string tension working against you near the fingerboard. Experiment with where you place your right hand, since each bass is different. To snap the string, get just the tip of the finger under the string and pull quickly with a snap of the wrist. The photos show how to pop on the D string with the first finger (Figure 7) and on the G with the second finger (Figure 8).

Figure 7.

Figure 8.

The following exercises involve snapping on both the *D* and the *G* strings. Use only the first finger to play each exercise, and then use only the second finger. Next, alternate fingers for each note (first finger, second finger, first finger, and so on). Remember, whenever you see a "P" above a note, pluck it either with your first or second finger.

Exercise 4.   *Exercise 5.*

Here are two ways of positioning the thumb while popping. Figure 9 shows the thumb pointing up, with the wrist raised off of the bass; Figure 10 shows the thumb pointing down with the wrist closer to the bass's body.

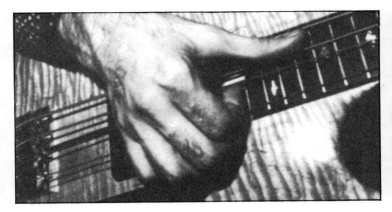

Figure 9.

Figure 10.

The next four exercises combine the thumb slap and the finger pop. They are straightforward, and only contain the techniques covered so far.

Exercise 6.   *Exercise 7.*

Exercise 8.   *Exercise 9.*

The following examples include two more techniques. The first is called a hammer-on, or slur. You probably use it already, but a popping style adds a whole new dimension to it. A hammer-on is executed by fretting a note with the left hand, plucking the string with the right hand, and then fretting a note higher on the same string (without moving the left hand from its original position). The "H" written above a note indicates that it should be hammered on:

For the example shown, use the 1st finger to press down the *D* (5th fret, *A* string), strike or pluck the note, and press down the 3rd or 4th finger on the 7th fret. This will produce the *E* note.

The second technique, called the undefined note, is not often used except as a rhythmic device. As the name implies, there is no clear pitch produced when you strike the string, but as with drums there is a relative pitch (high or low, in varying degrees). It is a good percussion sound, often used by the late Jaco Pastorius, Larry Graham, Stanley Clarke, and others. It appears on sheet music like this:

To play the undefined note, place a left-hand finger lightly upon the string at the note that corresponds to the "X" in the music; don't press the string to the fingerboard. Now snap or thumb the string with your right-hand thumb or fingers (a "T" or "P" above the note will tell you which to use). The first two examples here include only hammer-ons, but the third one makes use of the undefined note as well.

Exercise 10.   *Exercise 11.*

Exercise 12.

Naturally, you will want to go beyond mere exercises to vent your creativity. Try the following funk-style bass line. It should wet your feet and let you know what you're up against. Run through it at a comfortable pace until you get the technique under control: then worry about your speed. You won't always be afforded this luxury—on the bandstand or in the studio you must often be able to sight-read just about anything they give you. But for now, the idea is to learn the technique.

Exercise 13.

Exercise 13 (continued).

The final two examples illustrate bass popping in action. The first is the part that was given to me to play on a commercial. The second is the way I actually played the part after I renotated it with popping and additional fills. In the reworked part, I added the fills in bars 5 and 7. I removed the slurs between bars 1 and 2, and between bars 5 and 6. Notice the added hammer-ons in bars 4 and 8. This piece is just one example of how a bass part can be spiced up with popping.

Play both of the following examples as they are written, and you'll hear the difference. With time and experimentation, you will doubtless come up with many of your own. Try popping on the tunes you do with your band (preferably at a rehearsal—you never can tell if something will work for the first time at a gig).

Exercise 14.

Exercise 15.

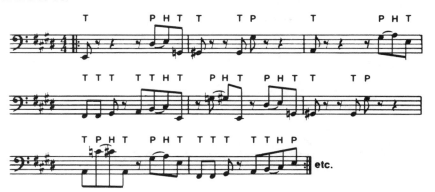

Here is a short list of records that feature bass popping techniques. You probably have other favorites, so listen closely to them, too.

By Ken Smith

A SELECTED
BASS POPPING DISCOGRAPHY

Larry Graham: (with Sly & The Family Stone) *Greatest Hits*, Epic, PE 30325; (with Graham Central Station) *My Radio Sure Sounds Good To Me*, Warner Bros., BSK-3175; *Star Walk*, Warner Bros., BSK-3322. **Charles Meeks:** (with Chuck Mangione) *An Evening Of Magic: Chuck Mangione Live At The Hollywood Bowl*, A&M, SP-6701. **Robert "Pops" Popwell:** (with the Crusaders) *Images*, ABC, BA-6030. **Stanley Clarke:** *I Wanna Play For You*, Nemperor [dist. by CBS], KZ2 35680; *Modern Man*, Nemperor, JZ-35303; *Journey To Love*, Nemperor 433. **Verdine White:** (with Earth, Wind & Fire) *I Am*, Columbia, FC 35730; *All 'N All*, Columbia, JC 34905. **Louis Johnson:** (with the Brothers Johnson) *Look Out For #1*, A&M, SP-4567. **Andy West:** (with the Dixie Dregs) *Free Fall*, Capricorn, CP 0189. **Marvin Isley:** (with the Isley Brothers) *Winner Takes All*, T-Neck [dist. by CBS], PZ2 36077. **Jaco Pastorius:** (with Weather Report) *Heavy Weather*, Columbia, PC 34418. **Alphonso Johnson:** *Yesterday's Dreams*, Epic, PE 34364.

The "In And Out" Technique

Guitar Player magazine August 1981

Figure 11.

Figure 12.

This technique promotes speed with *feeling* while playing sixteenth-note type bass patterns, such as the patterns in the following musical example. Using the tip of the finger, play the first note of the pattern *in* towards the body (Figure 11) and play the second note *out* from the body (Figure 12). Continue in the same manner until you reach the two consecutive eighth-notes. Each note of the eighth-note group is played *in*. Continue throughout the following music as an exercise at different tempos, to strengthen your finger and for comprehension of the "in and out" technique.

The string distance from the neck of the bass is important in making the "in and out" technique comfortable and practical for each individual. A musician who has a soft playing touch and/or soft nails should set the strings close to the neck. This puts the strings closer to the pickups for a soft touch and saves your nails from excessive wearing, tearing, and breaking. Use your discretion and logic when altering your equipment. If you have a strong touch and your nails do not break easily, it may not be necessary to lower your strings.

By Chuck Rainey

In And Out Exercise

The Slapping-Wood Technique

When you need to improvise a bass pattern, the sound of the notes can be altered to achieve melodic and/or rhythmic interest. The slapping technique produces a gutty, raunchy string-against-wood sound. It may also resemble a low percussive trombone or a musical grunt. The sound may vary, depending on the individual use of the technique, which involves a hand slap on the E string. The hand should be firm, but with its relaxed natural curvature.

As you slap the string with the extended fingers, the heel of the hand simultaneously hits against the top of the body of the bass. The extended fingers bounce right off the string naturally. The idea is to get the extended fingers to feel like one unit, supported by the wrist and controlled by the wrist muscles (like a drumstick in a drummer's hand).

When you slap, you should hear the note fingered, the string striking against the neck of the bass, and the complete value of the note intended. If the complete value of a slapped note is not achieved, consider the following check points: 1) hitting, banging, or slapping a note too hard can prevent the string from ringing its intended length; 2) string distance from pickups—the string may be set too far from, or too close, to the pickups; 3) type of strings you are using; 4) volume of bass; 5) volume of amplifier.

The slapping technique is used on the following albums: Aretha Franklin, *Young, Gifted And Black*, "Rock Steady" and "Border Song" (Atlantic Records, SD 7213); Quincy Jones, *Body Heat,* "If I Ever Lose This Heaven" (A&M Records, SP 3617); Quincy Jones, *You've Got It Bad,* "Sanford And Son Theme" (A&M, SP 3041); Quincy Jones, *Smackwater Jack*, "Theme From Ironsides"—bass solo (A&M, SP 3037); Roberta Flack, *Quiet Fire,* "Go Up Moses" (Atlantic, SD 1594).

Remember, sensitivity is necessary to attain the desired sound. Don't just hit, beat, or slap the bass without feeling. The following pattern can be used as an exercise to help you acquaint yourself with the feeling necessary from this technique.

By Chuck Rainey

Guitar Player **magazine March 1978**

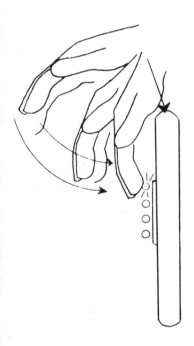

Slapping-Wood Exercise

◇ - **Wood symbol**

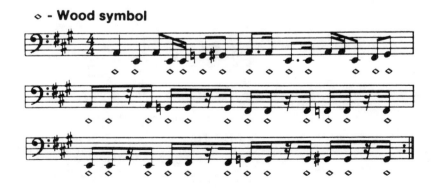

Finger Tremolo Technique

Guitar Player **magazine August 1975**

Sound creates style as much as technique. The four-bar segments of the three different bass patterns below can be played in many different styles by changing the *sound* of a few notes. By using a finger tremolo on the notes shown beneath the brackets, the pattern *feels* different, while maintaining its original structure.

The patterns indicated below are also explored in my mail-order course, *The Modern Bassist's Techniques Of Success*. This technique is also described in my book, *Disciple Of Emotion*. Make up your own patterns and experiment. Finger tremolos are used on the following tunes: "Shining Star," by Earth, Wind & Fire, on *Way Of The World* (Columbia Records, PC 33280); "Funk Freak," by White Heat, on *White Heat* (RCA, APL1-0853); "I Get Mad," by Joe Cocker, on *I Can Stand A Little Rain* (A&M Records, SP-3633); "You Are The World," by Donald Byrd, on *(High) Steppin' Into Tomorrow* (Blue Note Records, BN-LA 368-G).

By Chuck Rainey

Finger Tremolo Patterns

Tremolo played on 4th beat   T   = Tremolo

Tremolo played on 2nd and 4th beat

Tremolo played on 4th beat

The Left Hand

People have seen me play at live concerts or at conventions and invariably say, "You make all those licks that sound so hard, look easy." I find myself repeating, "It's in the hands—the hands!" Actually, a player can be fast, fluid, accurate, and mostly relaxed if he (or she) follows the basic outline below.

The trick is in using the left thumb as a pivoting home bass. The thumb points toward the nut of the neck and should be very close to the middle of the back of the neck. Equal pressure should be applied between each finger and thumb when playing a note. Normally, the thumb rides a little *behind* the 1st finger and if a note is up a little out of range, DON'T MOVE THE THUMB! Pivot (rotate) it so it thrusts the entire front part of your hand up (don't stretch the fingers) to reach that note. Keeping the thumb there helps you find your original position again. Most players tend to lift their left wrist up (this deters good hand position); keep the wrist down so that the fingers have access to the fingerboard. You don't need to play on the very tips of your fingers like a guitarist or violinist, nor as low as a string bass player either. Remember the electric bass requires an entirely different approach than the guitar or string bass.

Keep the front part of the left hand relaxed. Don't stretch except for the very fast notes. Play almost on top of the fret, let go of each note once you're on the next one. String bassists tend to hang onto notes too long and press too hard, as they are accustomed to heavy pressure. As you play up and down the neck, the thumb should usually follow the front part of the hand (like a caterpillar motion). It rarely jumps *with* the whole hand. This is where most players make their mistakes—they work too hard and lose their place easily. The more "up" on the neck the hand goes, the further "back" the thumb slides, so that when you jump to a lower note, the thumb jumps very little, while the hand can move almost an entire octave without missing a note.

I prefer not to use open strings because your impact is heavier and greater while playing closed positions. Open strings are good as fast time fillers (x-notes), or for special open ringing sounds, but otherwise timbre and playing ease suffer.

In this case, the fingering goes 1-2-4-4-4 (or, 1-2-3-4-4 on smaller necks) going up chromatically (leave the thumb there), and 4-2-1-1-1 (or 4-3-2-1-1 on smaller necks) going down chromatically; again, leave the thumb there. If something hurts, check to make sure your wrist is lowered and your elbow isn't clenched to your body—the arm should be relaxed. The 3rd finger may assist the 4th, and should be used on a note underneath the previous note on the same fret but on a lower string. For instance, play the following pattern:

Notice how the use of the 3rd finger makes the pattern flow better. Also, the 3rd finger may be a substitute for the 4th in the higher register. To strengthen each finger individually, I found two exercises which help:

1. Press equally hard with thumb against 1st finger several times. Then 2nd finger with the thumb, and so on. Pressing against a tennis ball is also good. Remember, only one finger at a time—you already have the natural "brute" hand strength you need. Strong 1st finger *dexterity* is what you're after now.
2. Close your fingers into a fist, pointing your thumb out and away from the rest of your hand. Now, without raising any other fingers, raise fingers 1 and 3 together (this is a "toughie" and if you get the 3rd finger up even a little, you're doing fine—it'll improve with practice), put them down in the closed position and then raise fingers 2 and 4 together. This exercise is also good for your concentration habit—take it easy at first. You'll have fun pulling it on your friends once you get

Guitar Player **magazine   June 1974**

accomplished at it. No fair cheating by holding your fingers down. This is a test I would give potential guitar students years ago, to see if they had coordination and concentration powers.

Guitar fingering (one finger per fret 1-2-3-4) is good only on small necks and scale-type patterns or jazz-type bebop solo work. The idea of the left hand is to keep it totally in a relaxed state at all times with the thumb as your pivot home base (or anchor). Most players almost give me a heart attack when they hook their left thumb over the neck as if to hang onto it—think how much more speed they'd have if they only knew!

By Carol Kaye

Right Hand Technique

Bass Player **magazine**
November/December 1988

Some aspects of the electric bass guitar are similar to the electric guitar: It is of comparable shape and size, and in its most common 4-string configuration, is tuned an octave below standard guitar tuning. It's easy to make the mistake of lumping them in the same category, but the different roles they play actually set them apart rather than together. In fact, its closest tonal relative, and the instrument the electric bass guitar was designed to replace and/or improve upon, was the standup bass, which has little, if any, relation to the guitar.

Most standup basses have the same basic construction and component part placement, so a bassist can rely on having a consistent anchor point to rest his or her thumb for plucking-finger strength. Because the instrument requires so much strength to pluck, you need to anchor your thumb in order to get the necessary leverage. String spacing is also generally consistent from one standup bass to the next, as the strings themselves are occasionally used as anchor points too.

But electric basses can be quite different from brand to brand. Many companies come up with new ideas about how to put together the instrument, but not always with an eye on how the instrument will be held and played in relation to any standard technique. Once you develop a technique on one kind of bass, it can sometimes require a major change in that technique to go to another type of bass, since dimensions and part placements can fluctuate wildly.

This problem doesn't seem as severe for picking techniques, or for that matter, thumb popping. But it's been my experience that many beginning players have trouble finding information on right-hand technique for fingerpicking electric bass. If they do have any technique, it is usually physically weak, with a lack of consistency in tone and note volume that would never hold up onstage or in the studio. I believe a bass should be played with strength, using the strings and the hands for the attack and tone, rather than relying on electronics. This lends itself to tonal individuality, since no two sets of hands are alike.

My purpose for explaining my right hand technique is not an attempt to suggest that it is *the* correct method. It's worked well for me, but may not be effective for another player. But I have had many other players tell me that it has been helpful, even if only to assist them in formulating their own technique, using mine as a foundation.

Here is an overview of the component parts of my right-hand technique, and the aspects of it that have helped other players:

Arm/Forearm (From The Shoulder Down). If you sit down while you practice, be sure to adjust your strap so that the bass is in the same position it usually is when you play standing up. *Don't laugh.* I've actually seen players burn away for hours in a dressing room, and then go onstage—changing the angle of every joint from shoulder to finger—and spend an entire set wondering why nothing works. This can also result in an extremely sore left shoulder.

Many times people will unconsciously compensate for a long strap by shrugging their shoulder to raise the bass. Take a close look at how you hold your instrument.

My forearm pushes the bass—at its highest contour—into my ribs, which are tucked into the indentation on the side of the bass' body (a traditional P-bass style). Every point of contact is utilized for the stability of my hands, as well as the stability of the bass on my body. The forearm may lift off for various moves, but it generally holds the bass up against me.

Wrist. Recently, a group of bass players told me that they were advised to keep their wrists limp and floating over the strings. Being limp-wristed is the last thing I would ever advise for anybody, especially bass players. To each his own, but I prefer locking my wrist to give my fingers a stable and strong foundation. That way you can get the most out of your strings by playing firm—with conviction, strength, and solidity. Save the light stuff for esoteric bass soloing. When you're playing bass in a band onstage, *clamp it down.*

Thumb. Primate mammals have opposable thumbs; that is, a thumb that opposes or pushes against the forefingers, allowing precise articulation and manipulation. To pluck a string, I anchor my thumb and pull one of my fingers toward it. The strength of the pluck is proportional to the firmness of the anchor.

My thumb touches three parts of the bass in its normal position: The low *E* string, the bridge side of the pickup (P-bass style pickup), and the pickguard or bass body underneath (see Figure 13). It moves to the top edge of the pickup when I play the *E* string, or all strings together (Figure 14), and it moves down onto the *A* string and pickup when playing the *D* and *G* strings (Figure 15). It's *always* anchored firmly, usually touching two or more points. I've seen bass players improve dramatically by attending to—and remedying—this one point alone.

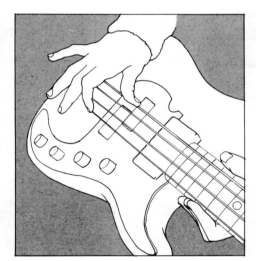

Figure 13.

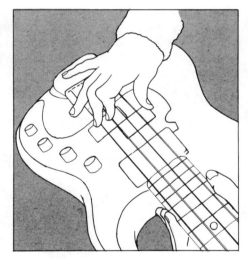

Figure 14.

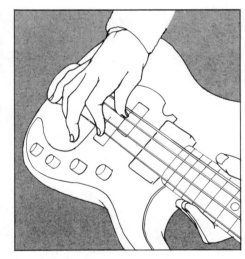

Figure 15.

Fingertips And Joints. Here we manipulate the actual sound of the strings. In order to get a good tone, it is advisable to develop a thick callus where your finger makes contact with the string. Extreme strength and endurance (and a high threshold for pain), will lead to well-callused fingertips. Also, a callus has a different drag coefficient than uncallused flesh when it passes over a string; like the difference between using a rubber eraser and a hard pick. The uncallused flesh grabs the string rather than percussively plucking it.

Another often overlooked aspect of fingering is deciding which joints of the finger are best suited as flexing points. There are three joints for each finger: The first, nearest the fingernail; the second, in the middle; and the third at the knuckle.

I keep the knuckle tight and straight, flexing from the second joint, leaving the first joint loose to rake over the string—bending backwards as it goes—while tightening or loosening the first joint to vary the strength of the attack. This is more effective than flexing from the knuckle, because the radius of the arc created by the movement of the shorter finger length (middle joint to fingertip), is smaller than the radius of the arc created by the similar finger movement from the knuckle to the fingertip. Therefore it can hit one string without hitting another in close proximity. The less you have to move, the less room there is for error. To take it to the extreme—imagine stiffening from shoulder to fingertip, laying your bass down, and plucking from the shoulder. Pretty inefficient.

That's a basic overview of right-hand technique as it applies to me and my playing. I hope that some of it may apply to you, and help you to establish a more comfortable, efficient approach.

By Billy Sheehan

Bass Fingering Techniques

Guitar Player **magazine August 1981**

About five years after I started playing the bass, I began to teach. My first students had been playing as long as I had, but wanted to learn about walking bass lines in jazz applications. Their problem was their lack of knowledge of the major scales; none of my students could play them 100 percent perfectly, and so they couldn't figure out chords in an accurate manner.

After teaching for a while, I found that I was going to have to learn several ways to explain music fundamentals in order to make things super-clear to the students. I started checking through a lot of music theory and harmony books in order to get my material together, and I also incorporated physical techniques that some excellent teachers had introduced to me. When physical problems (such as poor fingering technique) are corrected, a bassist can play easier and with a more organized conception of note location when sight-reading.

In the last 20 years I have taught a large variety of bass players from eight to 51 years old. Here are some observations I've made in that time: About 90 percent of the students playing electric bass are self-taught, and are barely able to read quarter-notes, even after five years on the instrument.

I would say that 95 percent of the people I see are struggling with guitar fingerings on the bass, and have no idea that there are other fingerings that are easier—especially for people with small and medium-size hands. Most of these people have memorized scales

Guitar Fingering
String Bass Fingering

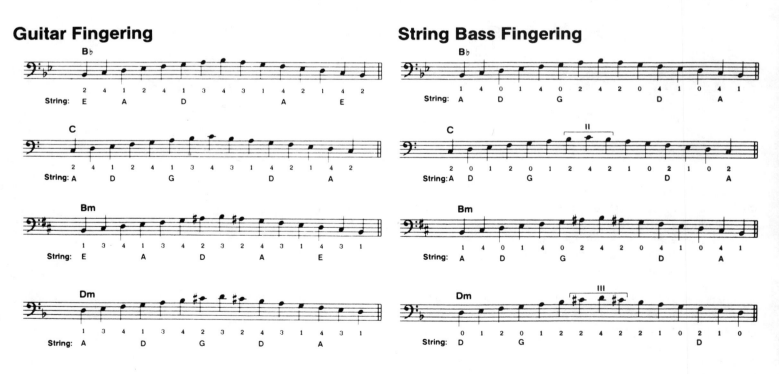

1 = 1st finger down on string
2 = 1st and 2nd fingers down on string
3 = 1st, 2nd, and 3rd fingers down on string
4 = 1st, 2nd, 3rd, and 4th fingers down on string
(notes under bracket are played within one position)

using certain fingering patterns that get them through the scales, but often they really don't know the names of each note they play. Consequently, this hangs up their reading.

There is a fingering technique that I use to teach; and after teaching it to over 2,000 bass players I know that it really works. The *Simandl* fingering is a system designed for string bass and uses the 1st, 2nd, and 4th fingers. The 3rd (ring) finger is not used independently in the low positions. For example, when playing a note with the 2nd finger, both the 1st and 2nd fingers are down on the string. When playing a note with the 4th finger, all four fingers are down on the string. This fingering covers three frets per position, instead of four—eliminating the stress of the four-finger stretch inherent to guitar fingering.

I feel this fingering works better for most people for three reasons: (1) The strings on an electric bass are thicker than those found on a guitar, and require more effort to push down; (2) the frets on a long-scale bass are farther apart than those on a guitar, and therefore the Simandl fingering will not be as strenuous as the four-finger guitar fingering; and (3) an electric bass' strings are farther apart than a guitar's.

A studio player generally must read without looking at his or her left hand, and the Simandl fingering system facilitates this. I have included below a few examples of scales comparing guitar-style and bass fingerings. Remember the following points, and you'll be playing the easiest way:

1. Keep a big space between the 1st and 2nd fingers; don't let the knuckles touch.
2. Keep the fingers curved—don't let the 2nd finger collapse.
3. Use your thumb as a pivot when going over to the low strings from the high strings (your elbows come forward, too). This helps to keep your fingers curved, and prevents flat-finger grabbing.
4. Practice in front of a mirror, so you can see your hand.
5. Don't take your hand off the neck when playing an open string.
6. Keep the 1st finger down when playing a note with your 2nd finger. Keep all four fingers down when playing a 4th-finger note.

By Herb Mickman

Stuart Hamm's Two-Handed Technique

Perhaps the most striking aspect of Stuart Hamm's style is his approach to two-handed playing. Rather than simply hammering on with his right hand as a mere embellishment, he uses it in much the same way as his left hand—sliding as well as fretting. In "Flow My Tears," from his solo album *Radio Free Albemuth*, he splits the repeating main melodic line between both hands. The first four notes of the music shown here are a left-hand part (written in bass clef and shown in Figure 16). Stuart says that they can be plucked with the right-hand fingers or thumb. All of the next eight notes are played by the right hand. The hand position for the first four treble-clef notes is shown in

Guitar Player **magazine August 1988**

"Flow My Tears"

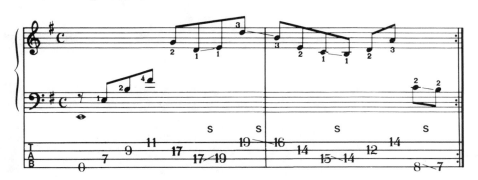

Figure 17. Hamm's right-hand position for the next three notes is illustrated in Figure 18. Three slides (indicated by a diagonal line with the letter "S") are performed in this series. The final two notes are a hammer-on and a slide, both created by the left hand.

By Tom Mulhern

Figure 16.

Figure 17.

Figure 18.

The Haslip Approach

Here are two examples of my approach to the bass. Figure 19 is taken from "Matinee Idol" on *Yellowjackets*. It shows a funk fingering and popping technique utilizing a classical-type picking approach for a bass played left-handed and strung right-handed. I use my left-hand 1st and 2nd fingers to fret the low notes, and my left-hand thumb to pop the higher notes. Note that "1" stands for the picking hand's index finger, "2" for the middle finger, "P" for plucked finger, and "T" for thumb hammering.

Figure 20 is taken from "Top Secret" on *Mirage A Trois*. It demonstrates a technique for using only the left-hand thumb for all the notes. The low notes and the high plucked ones are done with the thumb, and the slurring is accomplished with the fretting hand.

By Jimmy Haslip

Guitar Player **magazine February 1988**

Figure 19.

Excerpt From "Matinee Idol"   By Russell Ferrante

Figure 20.

Excerpt From "Top Secret"   By Jimmy Haslip and Russell Ferrante

The Wimbish Touch

Guitar Player magazine October 1987

Instead of using a method-book approach to right- and left-hand fingerings, Doug Wimbish opts for his own unorthodox but comfortable style. He uses a combination of different techniques for each type of music he plays. For basic playing, he favors a one-finger-per-fret-spacing, with his left-hand 1st finger acting as a capo or nut. He often uses his pinky when trilling, even if the trill is only a whole-step away. He plucks with one or two fingers, and although he's not against using a pick when it's called for, as it was with Mick Jagger, he prefers to use his fingernails for the same effect. Wimbish plays chords with his right-hand thumb and all four fingers, either in a fingerstyle motion or by striking the strings with the back of his hand and four fingers for a continuous, "galloping" effect.

For reasons of clarity, Wimbish's specialized techniques can be divided into three areas: thumb/hand slaps, harmonics, and tapping. For thumbstyle playing, he keeps his arm parallel to the floor and moves the entire arm in a reverse Frisbee-toss motion. As he does this, his wrist pivots toward his body, and his thumb—which is at a 75-degree angle—strikes the neck at the point where it joins the body. In the recoil motion, his fingers grab the top strings, pulling them outward. He likes to play drum rudiments, polyrhythms, and stop-time using his thumb on the low strings to simulate a kick drum and his fingers on the high strings to simulate the snare.

Applying harmonics is one of Wimbish's specialties, and he not only uses distortion as a way to bring them out, but tapping, two-handed slides, and heavy metal dive-bomb effects. For single-note harmonics, he uses the standard method of fretting a note with the left hand, while muting the string at the half-way point with his index finger and plucking the string with his thumb. He also applies the Jaco Pastorius method of locating the correct point with the thumb while pinching the string between the thumb and index finger. He slides harmonics on his fretless on one or more strings, and often expands upon these ideas by tapping.

While tapping techniques are gaining popularity every day through players such as Stanley Jordan and Billy Sheehan, Wimbish brings his own fresh approach to the art. He begins with a loose forearm, parallel to the ground, and a loose wrist angled down naturally from the arm so that when he taps all four strings, he produces an up-and-down motion like throwing a yo-yo. He taps the strings with the pads and first joints of his fingertips (not the tips), where he has developed hard calluses. His point of attack is right on the fret, which produces the clearest tone, although he sometimes strikes between the frets to add tone colors. Again he frets the desired note with his left hand and taps at the halfway point, dividing the string equally.

Wimbish's left-hand tapping is similar to his right in that he strikes the strings with his finger pads. But he taps the string *between* the frets and pulls his fingers away from the fingerboard with his thumb anchored on the neck, or he pulls his entire hand away if he is playing in more of a keyboard style.

From this point Wimbish begins his variations. Aside from using two-handed, ten-fingered taps to imitate drum flams and rolls, he employs both index fingers, alternately tapping a straight eighth-note figure on the same fret to simulate a sequenced bass line. He melodically lines up an arpeggio and reels if off, creating altered chords and progressions along the way. Moving back into harmonics, Wimbish mutes notes with his palm, unleashing lead lines. By fretting a G note with his left hand and rapidly tapping at the correct intervals down the string, and by hitting a low F note with his left thumb, he reproduces the overtone series while creating a rich polychord of G/F or F13#11. A favorite technique involves fretting a note with his left hand, tapping the harmonic with his right, and then bending the string and the one above it with his left hand. As the harmonic ascends to its peak, he taps the harmonic on the string above and lets that one descend, producing a provocative sound.

The key to Wimbish's style is the way he mixes all of his techniques while holding down the groove. He explains, "I can do all of them within four bars, or support an entire song, if I'm playing alone. I can provide the drums, melody, harmony, and bass parts."

A good example of several Wimbish effects at once occurs in what he calls the "flamenco slap." Illustrated in the musical example below, this involves a combination of techniques within a two-bar phrase. The figure on the first and third beats of the first bar and the first beat of the second bar involve tapping the *E* string at the base of the neck (see Figure 21). With his index finger and thumb positioned as if he were about to pinch the string, he taps the eighth-note and alternately taps, pulls outward, and taps the triplet figure. The second and fourth beats are both pulled outward with his thumb on the *E* string and his index and 2nd finger on the *D* and *G* strings, respectively (Figure 22), the difference being in the fingered notes for the left hand in beat two, as opposed to the barred harmonic at the 5th fret in beat four. The final two beats of the phrase involve two hands on the fingerboard (Figure 23).

He pulls out the *G* string with his right-hand index finger while playing a continuous hammer-on trill of the notes *D* and *E* with the 1st and 3rd fingers of the left hand. After triggering the trill, he shifts his right index finger to the *G#* on the *A* string and taps the syncopated ascending line, ending up in a good position to repeat the phrase by tapping the open *E* string again. It should be noted that to achieve the desired effect, the exercise must be played at between 144 and 192 beats per minute, the tempo at which Wimbish used similar drum-type licks in his onstage solo intro to "Lead Boots" with Jeff Beck. Playing it at any tempo will open you to new techniques and ideas, so start slowly!

Wimbish also suggests that you feel free to make harmonic changes, such as using different chords on the second and fourth beats or changing the ascending line to a descending one reading *D, C#, C,* and *B* on the *E* string. But he stresses the importance of thinking rhythmically first and foremost, pointing to the last two beats, where the two rhythms play off of each other. In this piece it is the rhythm that creates the motion and the interest.

By Chris Jisi

"Doug Wimbish Flamenco Slaps"

Figure 21.

Figure 22.

Figure 23.

Chapter 5:
Soloing

Soloing

Playing Solos

Guitar Player magazine January 1977

Playing solos on the bass, and taking the role of a lead-type player in a musical situation, is a very interesting subject. I am asked quite frequently about it, so I thought I would start this discussion by giving some of my ideas on lead playing.

The first thing I must do is explain the basic role of a bass player (one who usually plays a bass viol or an electric bass guitar). Just knowing the meaning of the word "bass" as defined in Webster's Dictionary—"an instrument of the lowest range"—it is very obvious that the first, most important thing for bass players to remember is that since their sound is of the lowest range, naturally they would have to handle that area in the music being dealt with. I know that sounds very simple, but it is very true.

Next in the role of bassists is what they do with that sound. Now what is usually done, and what's been going on for as long as I can remember, is that the bass player is one who acts as a harmonic stabilizer as well as a stabilizer of rhythm. In other words, if a bassist is playing a song that has three chords that repeat one after the other, each getting one beat—something like a *C* chord to an *F* chord to a *G* chord, etc.—the way to apply this idea of the bass' role is to play the roots of the chords *C, F,* and *G*. And at the same time the bassist plays each one of those roots on every beat it appears.

Of course, this can be altered to suit anyone's own particular taste—i.e. one could extend the range of the instrument by adding extra strings (which allows for a higher range to work with) or by playing notes other than the roots of chords, and so on. The possibilities are endless; however, I must stress that anyone who really wants to become a good bassist should have some idea of the role that goes along with the instrument. All the great bass players I've listened to extensively have had this "knowingness"—musicians such as Paul Chambers, Scott LaFaro, Richard Davis, Charles Mingus, Billy Cox, Noel Redding, Ron Carter, just to name a few.

I could go on forever about the role of the bass player, but this is enough for what we are going to cover here. How this fits into soloing as a bassist is very simple. If a bass player is using an electric, and is playing with, let's say, an electric piano, electric guitar, and drum, I've found it wise to alter the bass sound a bit for soloing (especially with these other instruments). Maybe make it "brighter" for the solos and then come back to the normal sound for ensemble playing. I've found that this helps me enormously when I'm peforming or recording. The problem that this overcomes is one of clashing timbres when, for instance, the timbre of the bass drum is directly in the range of the bass' timbre. All you need do to handle this is change the timbre of one of the two sounds. You'd be amazed at the difference just a very slight change will make.

As far as actual playing is concerned, if a bassists want to feel comfortable soloing they should familiarize themselves with whatever music they're going to be dealing with. If you are going to solo in a song that has chord changes like one bar of *A* minor to one bar of *D7* to two bars of *G* minor, you'd better know something about those chords—what the notes are in the chords, and what scales can be played from these chords.

Even more important is getting the overall feeling of the song. This can be accomplished by maybe playing the melody, or just simply listening to the song as a whole to get the concept of it, so you can have something to work off. When I was practicing a lot what I used to do to strengthen my improvising ability was sit down at the piano and play chords, write them down on paper or maybe just remember them, and make little exercises using the scales I knew were related to the chords. This sort of thing can also be done in almost the opposite way—I would get a scale I liked (and, boy, some of those scales were weird), then find the chords that would go along with the scale, and I'd write songs that way. For example:

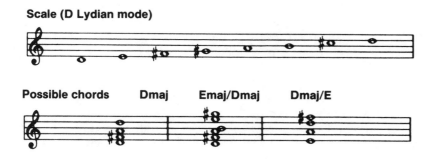

Scale (D Lydian mode)

Possible chords Dmaj Emaj/Dmaj Dmaj/E

A very important factor in all this is getting yourself to the point where you can *apply* this sort of stuff. Any piece of technical information is not fully understood in its fullest sense until it can be applied. Meaning: A person could remember all the notes of all the chords and scales in his or her head, and that's about as far as those scales and chords would go unless the musician applied them by playing and practicing and working with them until he or she could play them inside-out.

I used to sit down and listen to a lot of John Coltrane records and try to figure out what he was doing. I remember one song called "Out Of This World" [*The John Coltrane Quartet*, Impulse, 21] that was basically a very simple song with only a few chords to it. But I could never figure out how John could play so much stuff even within just one chord. So I listened and listened and finally came to the understanding that basically he was dealing with about eight notes related to the chord, and he was taking these eight notes and doing everything possible with them, playing them all in different sequences, and at the same time (underneath it all) making everything sound very melodic, and comprehensive to me. When I finally understood what he was doing, I applied what I had found, used it, and came up with all sorts of ways to play off the scales and chords in this song.

I have noticed that when bassists have a very good grasp of the music they are playing—being able to play it at will any way they wish to—they can create the greatest bass lines, can play the most creative solos, and are usually very happy about it. And the other musicians they are playing with are usually very happy, too.

By Stanley Clarke

Soloing Through Changes

Guitar Player magazine January 1989

One of a bassist's most valuable assets is a good harmonic sense. In addition to a well-trained ear, a well-rounded understanding of harmony and melody will set you apart from the rest. Since a lot of today's music doesn't offer the opportunity to hear players brilliantly solo over chord changes, I suggest going back and listening to some of the older recordings by Wes Montgomery, saxophonists Charlie Parker and John Coltrane, and trumpeter Miles Davis just to hear how the masters of improvisation dealt with chord changes. This frame of reference will benefit your playing in all styles of music.

Even though our primary responsibility as bassists is to lay down the foundation for whatever music we are playing, this does not exclude us from having to know what to do when it's time to solo. An understanding of scales and arpeggios will help you go through the changes and provide conceptual maturity. I find that there are certain patterns in chord changes that occur frequently; for instance, the II-V-I progression. It's everywhere. So let's take a look at a few examples: Figure 1 simply shows a II-V-I progression in the key of *C* with *Dm7* being the II chord and *G* being the V chord.

If these chord changes were put in front of you and you were asked to solo over them, what would you play? Well, as for the *Dm7*, an arpeggio comes to mind, either starting on the root and playing up the arpeggio or starting on the 7th and playing down (as in Figures 2a and 2b). Also the use of the scale for *Dm7* (Figure 3). Combined usage of the scale and arpeggio is also an interesting approach (Figures 4a and 4b).

The next few examples are just various ways to approach playing over these changes. You don't necessarily have to start on the root when playing changes, and one of the qualities of a good soloist is being able to distinguish the chords, even without accompaniment. Don't let the G# in Figure 5 scare you. Likewise, don't be intimidated by some of the other chromatic tones (Figures 6, 7, and 8), because even though these notes don't appear to be in the actual chord, remember that when you are improvising, *you* make the rules. Just don't abuse the privilege.

I hope that these examples spark your imagination and inspire you to experiment with playing over changes. Obviously, the more you try, the better you will become. Another interesting challenge is to pick any Charlie Parker sax solo and learn it, as the late Jaco Pastorius did with "Donna Lee." There is so much valuable information there, and learning those types of solos on bass simply upgrades the status of the bass as a solo instrument (as Jaco did). Of course, good taste in knowing what to play and when to play it is the key to being a great bassist.

By Nathan East

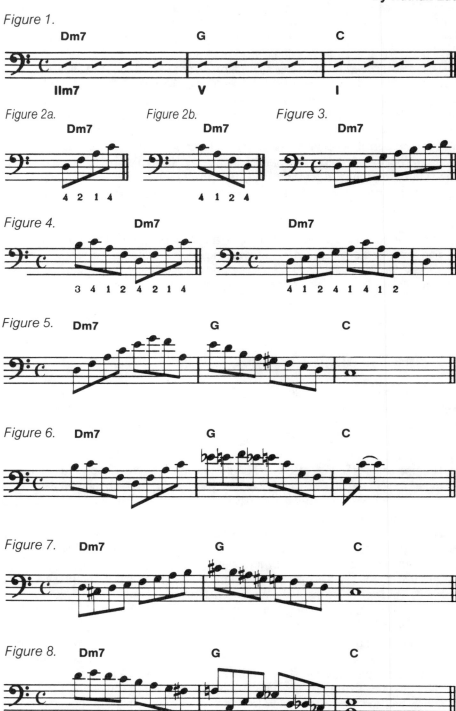

Playing Written Solos

I was pleased to get a call from Jimmie Haskell, a well-known arranger/composer here in L.A. He's got a resumé chock full of TV, album, and movie credits. Producers Michael Elias and Rich Eustis had given him the okay to write music for an ABC TV show originally titled *Dick And Tracy*, which was later renamed *Eye To Eye*.

Jimmie needed a bassist who read well and could play rapid sixteenth-note bass lines. This is almost unique, since studio bass parts are usually chord changes and "functionally correct" bass lines. We recorded at the Burbank Film Studios in Warner Brothers Soundstage No. 1 (the same soundstage where *Casablanca* was set to music).

This was the first TV show I ever worked on, but I had done a million commercials and other reading jobs, so the situation was basically the same. The great studio players who do this kind of music day-in and day-out are masters at sight-reading, playing with a strong time sense, playing with a click track (drummers are especially good at this), correcting sheet music, and—finally—changing their sounds on demand. This combination of abilities relates directly to *any* gig that you might get as a section musician with, say, Sammy Davis or Tom Jones.

The following is one particular bass part Jimmie wrote for me, a bass solo from bar 1 to the end. I was allowed 60 seconds to look it over, and one run-down before they hit the "record" button. We taped this cue at a metronome tempo of 148 beats per minute—each beat a quarter-note. No kidding. I'm glad I didn't know the tempo ahead of time, or I might have been even more nervous than I already was. The solo alternated between the written line and chord symbols, which I used as a basis for improvising. Knowing how to work from chord symbols is important because although you may not get calls to play fast music, you certainly can expect to alternate between notes and chord symbols. Learn the piece slowly, and then increase the speed so that you can get a feeling of the whole piece as a monument to bass panic.

By Jeff Berlin

Guitar Player **magazine August 1985**

Studio Date Sheet

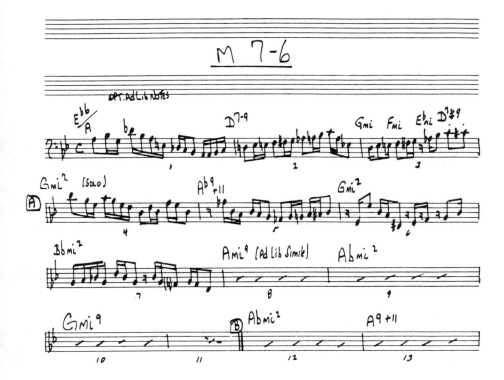

Soloing On "Latin"

Guitar Player **magazine August 1986**

Instead of giving you a transcription of my bass solo on "Latin" [from *Ivanhoe*, Inner City, IC 1162], I thought that it would be more interesting to show you which modes or scales I used to play my solo, so that you will be able to create your own phrases and later use the system for other tunes that present similar chords. The tune is very simple, and it's very good for practicing the Lydian modes.

The Lydian mode is built on the 4th degree of the major scale. In other words, if you play a *C* major scale starting from *F* (that is, *F, G, A, B, C, D, E, F*), you are playing *F* Lydian. If you play a *D* major scale starting from *G* (*G, A, B, C♯, D, E, F♯, G*), you are playing *F* Lydian. This is the case with all the major scales; again you start on the 4th degree.

The first chord of the solo is a *Dm11*, over which you play the *D* Dorian mode (built on the 2nd degree of the *C* major scale, or *D, E, F, G, A, B, C, D*). All the other chords are maj7 chords or maj7♭11 chords, over which you play the Lydian modes.

If we had to determine an order for which modes to play over a major 7th chord, I definitely would say the Lydian should be the first option, and the major scale itself only as the second option. (Of course, for the maj7#11, it is definitely the Lydian mode, due to the raised 11th.)

To play with these modes, you are not limited to the one octave that I have written on the chart, and also you don't have to start with the first note of the mode. You can start phrasing from any note within the mode. It should be not only a pretty easy exercise, but also an enjoyable one.

By Bunny Brunel

"Latin"

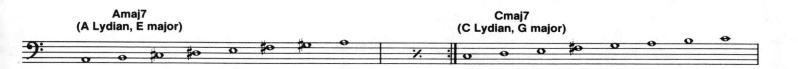

Index finger of right hand holds F#
whole chord with 4th finger of right

ridge

Chapter 6:
Progressions, Patterns & Bass Lines

Progressions, Patterns & Bass Lines

Variations In Blues

Guitar Player magazine May 1988

Sometime in your career as a bassist, you will find yourself in a situation where you must know how to play the blues. This is a simple task for most pros, but even still, there are so many different variations and feels, tempos, and so forth, that it can sometimes be difficult to interpret the music correctly.

Time signatures are big variables. While some blues songs are in 3/4 time, many are also in 6/8 or 12/8. Plus, the various feels range from bebop jazz to shuffle or rock. Sometimes a blues progression sounds happy using major chords (if that makes any sense—happy blues?), as opposed to the serious, down-in-the-dumps, depressed, heartbroken effect that can be achieved by using all minor chords at a very slow tempo.

Let's take a look at a shuffle feel, using the key of G in 4/4 time. Even in this one feel, there are several variations within the framework. Figure 1 shows the standard approach, a walking bass line that moves to the IV chord in bar 5 and back to the I chord in bar 7, with the V-IV-I cadence giving you your basic 12-bar blues progression.

Figure 2 uses the same basic progression with a more rhythmic approach. Don't let the F♮ in bar 1 throw you, even though it contradicts the key signature. Such a clash might not get past your theory teacher, but he'll get over it.

Figure 3 is yet another variation using substitute chord changes within the 12 bars. This particular set of changes is sometimes referred to as the "New York changes." It's quite a refreshing variation to use during a solo—for instance, as a slight departure from the repetitious, normal 12-bar pattern. Since the nature of a blues progression is to repeat over and over, it's good to try coming up with parts that keep the bass line interesting. In all types of music, it's important to figure out ways to keep the song building or growing.

Figure 4 is yet another way of moving a progression along, using our old friends, the double-stops. They seem to lift the whole ensemble from the bottom. I love when that happens: It makes the bass player look good!

By Nathan East

Figure 1.

Figure 2.

Figure 3.

Figure 4.

II-V-I Walking Bass Patterns In Minor Keys

Here are some variations of walking bass lines over a chord progression called the II-V-I in harmonic minor keys. In order to clarify the principles behind this and to help you understand the examples, I will first go over a few musical fundamentals.

Each note of the major scale is assigned a corresponding Roman numeral that indicates its scale step, or *degree*; see Figure 5. If we build a series of four-note chords using *only* the notes contained in that scale, we get a group of *diatonic,* or scale-tone, 7th chords; see Figure 6.

If you employ the idea of superimposed scale tones in a harmonic minor scale context, the result is similar to that in Figure 7. If we build a series of diatonic triads on that scale, the results are like those in Figure 8. In Figure 9 we see the effects of building up four-note chords based upon a harmonic minor scale.

One of the most common chord progressions in minor keys (or in parts of songs that modulate to a minor key) is the II-V-I; see Figure 10. In harmonic minor, the II chord is a half-diminished 7th (a minor 7th chord with a lowered 5th). The V is a dominant 7th, and the I chord is a minor/ major 7th (a minor triad with a major 7th interval).

Now let's look at some different approaches to creating a walking bass line to use with these chords. Figure 11 contains 20 bass lines that show how to maintain the sound of the chord progression while playing a quarter-note pulse. Patterns A through E in Figure 11 all include chordal tones, while F and G are based on scales. Parts H, I, and J employ only chord tones, while pattern K is more melodic and departs from the use of roots on the downbeats.

Herb Mickman

***Guitar Player* magazine March 1981**

Figure 5.   *Figure 6.*

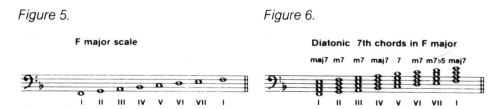

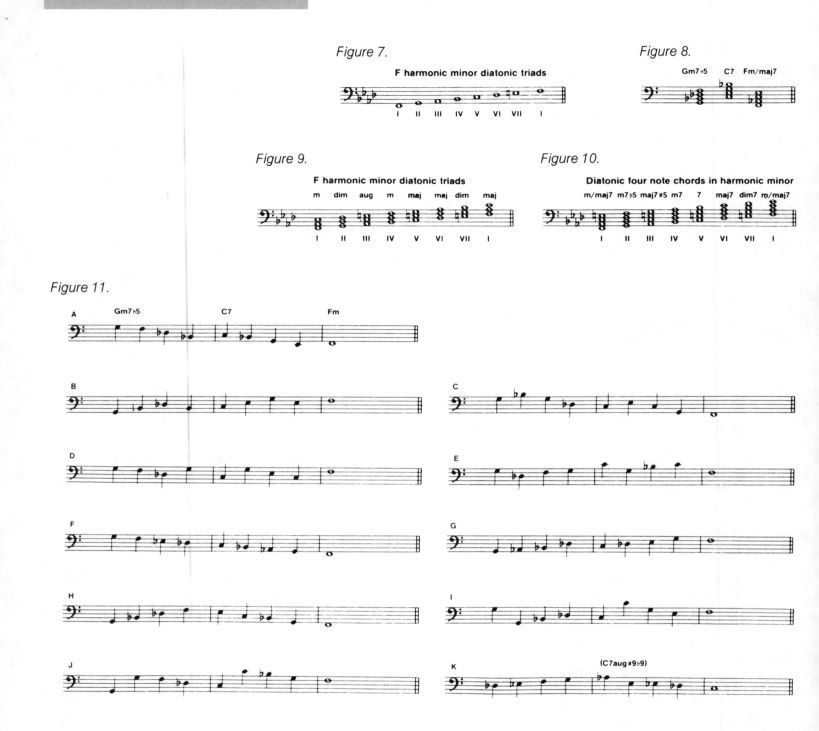

Figure 7.

F harmonic minor diatonic triads

I   II   III   IV   V   VI   VII   I

Figure 8.

Gm7♭5   C7   Fm/maj7

Figure 9.

F harmonic minor diatonic triads

m   dim   aug   m   maj   maj   dim   maj

I   II   III   IV   V   VI   VII   I

Figure 10.

Diatonic four note chords in harmonic minor

m/maj7   m7♭5   maj7#5   m7   7   maj7   dim7   m/maj7

I   II   III   IV   V   VI   VII   I

Figure 11.

A   Gm7♭5   C7   Fm

B   C

D   E

F   G

H   I

J   K   (C7aug#9♭9)

Bass Turnarounds

Guitar Player **magazine November 1985**

I look at music as sound that takes place in time, is governed by time, created by time, in time (tempo). Listen to the "song" that a train plays while rumbling down the tracks. Tasteful timing makes good music and controls the flow and intensity of it, just as good training makes for excellence in performance. Knowing the *why* and *when to* of doing things is the key to becoming the great accompanist that every musician should strive to be. The *how to* comes from listening. First, you must learn to listen ahead, in order to anticipate what is coming, so that you can create the desired support for the lead instrument or vocal, while simultaneously listening to yourself and the other musicians to see how your part fits into the big picture. At the same time, you want to be flexible enough to change your part instantly in reaction to what you see and hear.

One of the best examples of the art of timing and listening is found in the creation and playing of *turnarounds*, or transitional phrases. Turnarounds occur in the last two bars of a verse and act as a transition to the chorus or the next verse. They can happen so often that there is a tendency to run out of ideas or to be intimidated by their importance. Try looking at them as a series of staircases leading to the different floors of the musical edifice you are constructing. Be aware that it isn't necessary to play something different at every turnaround. When playing the melody portion of an arrangement, one turnaround used over and over can become another primary element in the song. Most pop, rock, R&B, and blues bass lines use this concept of repetition. You might want to select a few turnarounds to put to work for an entire song. Now, you can employ a rhythmic/melodic approach (a fill) to create a turnaround, or you can use a harmonic/rhythmic approach (a pick-up and/or lead-in), or a combination of both—anything to create excitement or interest, stir things up, keep things going, bring things to an end, etc. In other words, you want to create *motion*. Sometimes this motion comes from the original line itself, and then there is no need for anything new to be added.

How do you approach the turnaround? For example, we're playing the introduction to Duke Ellington's "Satin Doll," and we've reached the turnaround (*Em7* to *A7*). Think "staircase." Do you run down the stairs, slide up the banister (musicians are magicians), or walk up one step at a time smoothly, or peg-leg (in an uneven gait)? Do you continue using the same line or something new? At this point (the intro), what do you want to say in order to introduce the melody? Decisions, decisions, decisions! Ask yourself: "Was the preceding portion dramatic, amusing, somber, or exciting—and in what style?"

Now that you are acquainted with some of the artistic considerations, let's get into the "skill" side of *what to*—as in what to play. From an accompanist's standpoint, *what to* concerns *harmonic propulsion* and *rhythmic drive*. For instance, we start out in the intro of a 12-bar blues; we're playing in a swing feel, straight four on the bass, and then we reach the turnaround. If you don't listen and think ahead, you might run out of ideas, since the I7 chord is employed for both bars of the turnaround in traditional blues. Working within this tight framework challenges creativity. Walk up the I7 chord using part of the blues scale (root, third, fourth, lowered fifth) and down the I7 starting on the 5th (fifth, fourth, third, second) using the major scale to lead to the first floor, or the verse.

Now we're at the last two bars of the first verse (the turnaround). Walk up the I7 chord (root, third, second, fourth), and continue walking up from the 5th of the I7 (fifth, sixth, lowered seventh, natural seventh), using the major (fifth and sixth) and chromatic (lowered seventh and natural seventh) scales to put you on the second floor (the verse) in a higher register. At the end of the second verse, walk down from the higher register (tonic, lowered seventh, sixth, lowered sixth) using chord tones (tonic and lowered seventh) and the chromatic scale (sixth and lowered sixth) to the 5th; continue walking down (fifth, fourth, third, second), leading to the third floor.

So far, we've played three turnarounds using only harmonic propulsion to create motion. Now, we're going to add rhythmic drive. The rhythm is the eighth-note triplet divided long-short (also thought of as a triple-let):

This rhythmic alteration should be played only on the first beat of the I7 turnaround, so that you have rhythmic and non-rhythmic interpretations of each of the three turnarounds, thereby making a total of six new turnarounds (2 x 3 = 6; by combining rhythmic and melodic patterns, a few concepts can be multiplied into an astonishing number of actual turnarounds). Now, if you do the same thing to the last bar of the I7, you will have three more rhythms times three harmonies, which equals nine turnarounds. Suppose you were to alter each beat so that each triplet is grouped with the first two notes tied together. You would then have eight different rhythmic patterns:

These eight rhythmic schemes multiplied by three harmonic patterns equal 24 turnarounds. In reality, if you use every possible combination of those eight beats, you'll have 64 rhythmic variations ($8^2 = 64$, or $8 \times 8 = 64$), such as altering beats one and eight, one and seven, one and six, etc.; two and eight, two and seven, two and six, etc.; and three and eight, three and seven, three and six, etc. By multiplying the 64 rhythmic patterns by three harmonic versions, you have 192 turnarounds. And we're just getting started! The ability to make changes in turnarounds is a must for supporting, setting up, inspiring, and moving the "new" music during the solo or instrumental sections of a piece.

Now that we've gotten this far, let's go back and simplify and summarize our thoughts on this *what to* skill. Each eight-beat harmonic line has 64 rhythmic interpretations that use just one rhythm! Let's now add extra rhythmic drive, a full eighth-note triplet and a triplet with an eighth-note followed by two eighth-notes tied together:

With these three, you will have a total of 192 (3×64) versions of each turnaround line, and if you combine them, you'll have a huge number. So, for the three turnaround lines, we can say there are at least 576 (3×192) variations. Now, suppose you combine the three turnaround lines harmonically. Four of the six turnaround measures were completely different; the other two were repeats of the pattern that uses the progression of the fifth, fourth, third, and second. These four different bars yield 16 different harmonic interpretations, so we're really saying 2,072 (16×192) versions derived from three harmonic lines using the eighth-note triplet. Need I say more? Okay, I will. If you use the other divisions of the basic beat—two eighth-notes, four sixteenth-notes (halves of eighth-notes), and their combinations, you will have seven more rhythms, bringing you to a total of ten:

With this, each harmonic line will have 640 (10×64) rhythmic variations, and in this case the 16 harmonic possibilities times the 640 rhythmic variations yields 10,240 possible turnarounds. Needless to say, the point here is not that you should atttempt a computer-like memorization of thousands of turnarounds, but rather that you should be aware of the enormous variety of combinations awaiting your exploration.

Now that we have a good idea of *what to*, and know that there is plenty of it, let's talk about the effect that certain rhythms and harmonies have on turnaround phrases. Knowing this will make the *how to* and the *why* and *when* closer to your actual feelings, allowing you to crystallize your self-expression and make an accurate statement.

The use of the monotone (one note repeated, which provides relief when you're tired) creates tension and dynamics when played as quarter-notes (see part *a* in the following figure). When played as eighth-notes (*b*), you add excitement, and the dynamic aspect becomes more dramatic. As eighth-note triplets (*c*), you build a climax of a lighter mood.

As sixteenth-notes (d), you create a riveting intensity along with the dramatic and exciting aspects of the eighth-note.

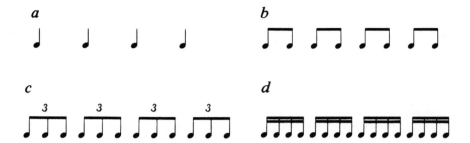

The same holds true for melodic lines, which use more than one tone. Therefore, when you're composing a turnaround or any melodic or harmonic line, think of the feeling that you're trying to create, and then apply the appropriate rhythmic grouping.

The use of many notes creates free motion, as in the jazz and classical styles; using fewer notes in a rhythmic pattern tends to lock—to create a groove, or a patterned sense of motion, as in R&B, Afro-Caribbean-Latin, and rock and roll. Pop music can be anything from a strong blend of all styles to a watered-down version of just one. It is most important to learn all styles of music *in their purest forms*. Each has a different sense of *why, when to,* and *what to,* but the *how to* is always the same.

In reality, every time the bass changes a chord, it's creating a turnaround because harmonic changes naturally create turnarounds within themselves and readily become part of the melodic structure as one change leads to the next; such is the case of the II V7 I progression and the first ten bars (I7 I7 I7 I7 IV7 IV7 I7 V7 IV7) of a 12-bar blues. Since the last two bars of the blues (I7 I7) are the same as the first four, you have to supply the harmonic propulsion through your own melodic creativity. Here are a few examples using the overworked II V7 I progression and the challenging I7 to I7 progression that yields over 100,000 different turnarounds when combined harmonically and altered rhythmicaly 320 ways for the 14 one-bar phrases (four beats) based on the I7 progression, and 640 ways in the case of eight two-bar phrases (eight beats) based on the II V7 I progression. Note: The arrows mean whether the following note is above or below the one preceding it.

14 x 14 harmonic phrases x 320 rhythmic alterations = 62,720

I7					I7			
1	3	4	#4		5	6	b7	7
1	↓7	6	b6		5	4	3	2
1	3	4	2		5	3	6	5
1	6	5	6		4	3	2	b2
3	5	2	1		↓3	6	5	3
3	1	4	2		5	7	2	5
3	4	4	5		6	5	b5	4

8 x 8 harmonic phrases x 640 rhythmic alterations = 40,960

IIm7		V7		I			
1	5	3	3	1	7	6	5
3	5	3	5	1	6	5	2
1	3	1	3	1	3	4	5
1	↓7	3	2	5	4	3	2
5	7	2	3	5	6	5	3
3	1	1	↓1	3	4	5	7
1	↓1	4	↑4	7	5	2	b2
3	2	5	4	1	6	5	4

Here are the 10 divisions of a single beat:

Bassists should learn to build chords and arpeggios using any of a chord's notes as the lowest. For example, the first inversion of a major chord is spelled out 3 5 1 (3rd, 5th, root). Using the *E* string to play a chord's 3rd, build the chord 3 5 1 3 5, lowest to highest. Do the same thing using the second inversion (starting with the chord's 5th as the lowest note): 5 1 3 5. Then try 3 5 1 3 5 1 and 5 1 3 5 1 3, using the *E* string to play the 3 and 5, as well as the 5 and 1. Add the 7th to the patterns, and listen to the melodies being formed.

Here are a few written examples derived from patterns in the blues shuffle, traditional jazz, rock, R&B and Afro-Caribbean-Latin styles (1 3 4 #4 and 5 6 ♭7 ♮7 over two bars of the I7 chord, and 1 5 3 3 and 1 7 6 5 over two bars of the II V7 I progression). Play the progression slowly as quarter-notes to get familiar with their sound. In a few cases, I've employed the monotone to create tension and additional harmonic propulsion when connecting the phrases. You, too, should think of the "main" notes of a phrase as landmarks, and use harmonic propulsion to satisfy the rhythm you're using to connect the phrases.

The blues shuffle and traditional jazz both employ some form of the eighth-note triplet for rhythmic drive. Take note of the placement and frequency of the rhythmic drive of these two styles. Rock generally employs the eighth-note and simple harmony, often based on the blues. R&B style generally relies on some form of the eighth-note and sixteenth-note rhythms with additional harmony to support these rhythms; whereas the Afro-Caribbean-Latin style employs the same rhythmic elements in a more relaxed but syncopated fashion with inverted harmonies. Within each of the two-bar phrases, either bar can be crossmatched with bars from other examples for more possibilities. In most cases, you can create a six-bar vamp by playing the two preceding measures, the two turnaround measures, and the I chord for the two measures in the same rhythm as the two preceding measures.

Very often, one is inspired and forms a new melodic/harmonic idea based on an existing one—by reinterpreting the original idea, or unconsciously altering it, or misinterpreting it. But as a result, a unique new idea may be formed that might suggest substitute or additional harmony. You *want* these kinds of variations to blend harmoniously. However, you might want to change the original idea altogether to make the best musical statement.

Additional information on turnarounds and improvisation can be found in my forthcoming book *Studies In The Art And Skill Of The Professional Bass Player*, as well as in Chuck Sher's *The Improviser's Bass Method* [Sher Music Co., Box 40742, San Francisco, CA 94140] and David Baker's *The Blues* [Chas. Colin Pub., 315 W. 53rd St., New York, NY 10019]. Listen to some of your own favorite musicians to observe how they handle turnarounds.

These turnarounds aren't just abstract ideas without basis in reality either. In fact, some of my favorite recordings on which I performed use many of these turnarounds. These include B.B. King's *Live & Well* [ABC, 819] and *King Curtis Live At The Fillmore West* [Atlantic, 40214]. Notice on the cut "Why I Sing The Blues" that I play a different turnaround with few exceptions for 20 verses, and change from locked time to free time on the 16th verse. With King Curtis on "Memphis Soul Stew," it's the V7 all the way, and I play a lead-in approximately every four bars to create a turnaround. On the late Jaco Pastorius' "(Used To Be A) Cha-Cha," from his first solo album, *Jaco Pastorius* [Epic, PE-33949], notice how he used lead-ins and fills to create the turnarounds throughout the piece, especially during the vamp at the end. Also listen to the simple rhythmic figure at the turnaround of Ashford & Simpson's "Solid" [*Ashford & Simpson*, Capitol, ST 12366]. Notice the simplicity of the turnarounds used in Lionel Ritchie and Michael Jackson's "We Are The World" [*We Are The World*, Columbia, USA-40043]:

With the art and skills of *how to* (by listening), *why* and *when to* (style, taste, and timing), and *what to* (your vast musical vocabulary and magicianship), you will be able to create the necessary turnaround with courage, confidence, and conviction.

By Jerry Jemmott

Bass Turnarounds

Traditional Jazz
The preceding two measures

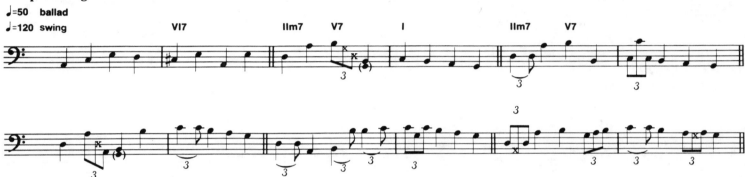

Rhythm And Blues
The preceding two measures

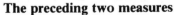

Rhythm And Blues Ballad
The preceding two measures

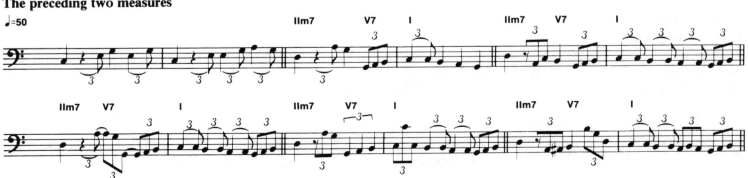

Afro-Caribbean-Latin
The preceding two measures

Blues Shuffle
The preceding two measures

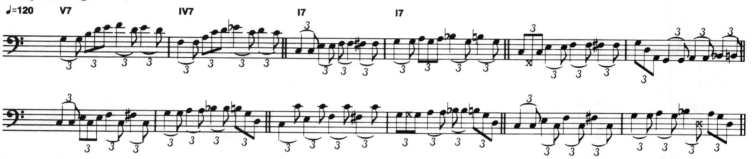

Traditional Jazz
The preceding two measures

Rock
The preceding two measures

Rhythm And Blues
The preceding two measures

Funk Bass Lines

Funk music is great. I especially love funk bass players and funk drummers. When two great funk specialists get together, feet aren't still, heads aren't still, and bodies twitch like they've been zapped with 10,000 volts. And it's all good for you, too.

Here's an idea to help you find some funky bass lines for yourself. First of all, the title of "funk" has a much wider meaning than it used to. Prince is considered funk. So are James Brown and Earth, Wind & Fire. But for now, let's stick to the Tower Of Power syncopated style of funk. If you read music, simply transfer the instructions not onto music paper, but into a cassette machine as you do the exercise verbally. Have a metronome going at around 48 beats per minute while you sing your parts. This way you can separate your rhythm decisions from the actual downbeat your metronome has provided.

Okay, let's begin our funk recipe. First of all, take 16 sixteenth-notes. This adds up to a full 4/4 bar.

Now randomly keep some of the notes and replace the others with sixteenth-note rests. You can choose any amount of rests and notes. Here are my random choices.

The non-reader might try to assign a verbal sound for the notes you keep, such as a hard spoken "Dot" to represent the missing notes, you might attempt a softly uttered "Pooh." It may seem silly, but give it a chance. Your tape should come out sounding something like, Dot Dot Pooh Dot Pooh Dot, etc. Just make sure that all together you have uttered 16 sounds in order to complete a 4/4 bar.

Next, put your example into a musically readable fashion (looking like a drum part). Combine sixteenth-notes and sixteenth-note rests only if they lay in a four-note grouping. Look at this example:

The non-readers should now pick up their basses and listen to their tapes. Play one note on your instrument and learn to play only the Dot portion of your verbal example. You may need a few passes. Listen to the metronome on the tape and work on isolating only the Dot sound and playing each Dot on your bass.

Finally, it's time for you to assign certain pitches to the rhythms we've used, just as a composer would do. Written below are the note choices I made to work with the rhythm line I came up with.

Guitar Player **magazine June 1986**

This method of funky line-writing should enable you to come up with many variations of bass lines. If you consider the other possibilities in 3/4, 6/8, 7/4, 5/8, and so forth, you have ample opportunity to amaze your friends and foes alike by demonstrating what a funky individual you really are.

By Jeff Berlin

Patterns With Chord Progressions

Guitar Player **magazine March, April 1987**

Sometimes the improvising bassist is required to learn songs quickly by ear. This musical skill improves with on-the-job experience and from repetition of various chord progressions. Our ears get used to certain sounds, enabling us to find the bass notes very fast. Naturally, the ability varies from player to player.

I've found that a good memory and a lot of knowledge helped me even more, since my ear wasn't very well-developed in the early part of my career. However, I started to see that there were some common chord progressions, and soon my ear "digested" them. Then I heard a trumpet player practicing sequences (patterns) with chords. What he played sounded easy and logical, so I tried it. It wasn't as easy as I had anticipated, but as I spent more time on it, my ear improved. So I decided to make up some other patterns and practice them on all kinds of chords, in all keys. It's been a lifetime study!

To do the following patterns, you must first understand chord inversions. An inversion is basically a different arrangement of a chord's notes so that the root is not necessarily on the bottom. If the root is the bottom note, the chord is said to be in *root position*. If the chord's 3rd is lowest, it's in first inversion. And if the 5th is the bottom, then the chord is in second inversion. Finally, if the 7th is the bottom note, the chord is in third inversion. Take a look at Figure 12 to see the differences between these inversions. Most of us have seen chord symbols with a line under the chord's name. The note on top or to the left of the line is the name of the chord, while the note below the line (or to the right) is the desired bass note.

In Figure 13, we see an *F7* chord (a dominant 7th), and there is a bar with an exercise to be repeated until it's memorized. Figure 14 is in the first inversion, Figure 15 is in second inversion, and Figure 16 is in third inversion. Play these until you have them memorized, and then write out the inversions for all the other dominant 7th chords. Practice them, too, until you have them memorized.

Figure 12.

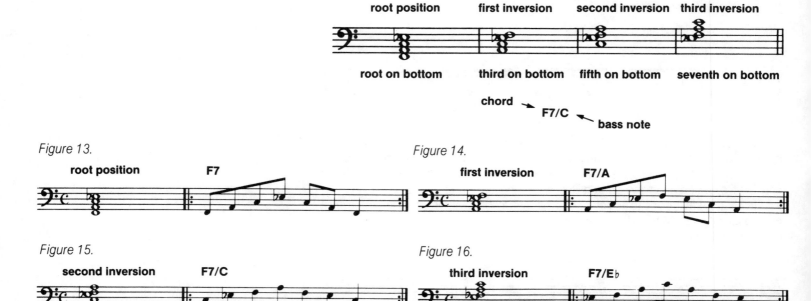

The patterns in Figure 17 use root-position dominant 7th chords. We begin by going up an *E7* and down an *A7*, but only using the 3rd and root of the *A7*. Play the first bar over until it's memorized, and be sure you're not doing it completely by ear—know the notes! The second bar is an *F7* to *Bb7*, and so on. The pattern goes up chromatically until you reach the high *E7* to *A7*; then it comes down, finally ending on *E7* to *A7*. Read it many times and listen to the sound of the chords; then memorize the exercise.

Figure 17.

When I was taking harmony class in high school, I was just becoming aware of chords built on the tones of the major scale. They're called *diatonic triads*, and are all illustrated in Figure 18. In this instance, the chords are built on the scale tones in the key of *C* major. Notice that the I, IV, and V chords are major triads. The chords built on the II, III, and VI are minor triads, and the chord built on the VII—the seventh note of the scale—is diminished. This pattern of major and minor triads is the same in the other keys and should be memorized.

I learned a valuable lesson in my harmony class—simply that there are several very common patterns that chords follow in songs. One of the most common progessions involves the II chord (a minor triad) moving to the V chord (a major triad). See Figure 19a.

I started to check out a lot of popular music, and I found II, V, I progressions in almost every song. I drew up a little chart of II, V, I progressions (Figure 20) and memorized it. Over the years it has proved invaluable. My ear developed, I became more experienced, and soon I could hear a II, V, I progression coming up in a song.

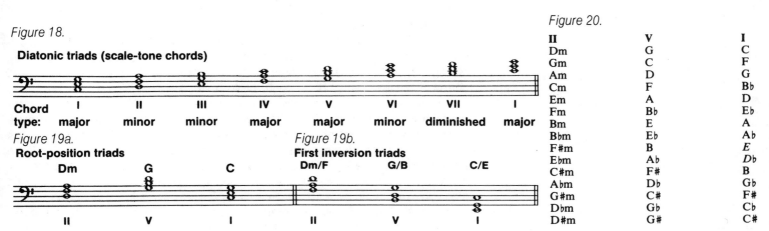

Figure 18.

Figure 20.

Figure 19a.

Figure 19b.

II	V	I
Dm	G	C
Gm	C	F
Am	D	G
Cm	F	Bb
Em	A	D
Fm	Bb	Eb
Bm	E	A
Bbm	Eb	Ab
F#m	B	E
Ebm	Ab	Db
C#m	F#	B
Abm	Db	Gb
G#m	C#	F#
Dbm	Gb	Cb
D#m	G#	C#

To get more familiar with the chord notes and chord progression, I've made up two effective exercises. In Figure 21 we start with *Em, A, D*—the II, V, I progression in the key of *D* major—and ascend chromatically, playing every II, V, I combination up the the II, V, I in *D* an octave higher. Then we descend chromatically, ending with the same three chords we began with.

Figure 22 utilizes first-inversion triads (Figure 18b shows their structure). This means that each triad has the 3rd of the chord as its bottom note. While the notes in each of Figure 21's arpeggiated chords ascend, the notes in Figure 22 *descend*. Play through these exercises many times until you've memorized them.

Figure 21.

By Herb Mickman

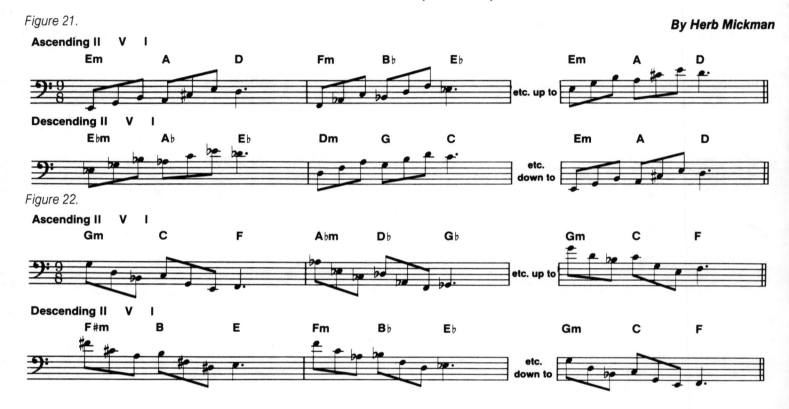

Figure 22.

Happy Endings

Guitar Player magazine July 1988

For all the time musicians put in creating, learning, and otherwise working with songs, all too often a song's ending gets a second-class treatment. The following examples take a look at some ideas for song endings. Perhaps you'll find that you have already heard or played some of these, but in any case they do come in handy, especially if you want to finish a song with something a bit more interesting than a held chord or just a simple cut-off. In classical music, the final phrase is called a *cadence*. An example of this is shown in Figure 23. In contrast, Figure 24 is a modern show-type ending that we have all heard and probably used fairly often. This is known as your basic, standard, on-cue, works-every-time ending.

Figure 25 is yet another familiar standard ending that can be used at the end of a swing/blues progression (I even heard this type of ending on an early Prince record). Most guitarists have dozens of variations on final phrases, and it's great to listen and borrow, if you like. Remember, though, a little goes a long way.

I've picked up a few good ideas along the way—for example, the ending of "Crossroads" from working with Eric Clapton. When we play it live, it's similar to the example shown in Figure 26. The ending that we use onstage for "Further On Up The Road" looks like Figure 27. Note the arpeggios in Figures 28, 29, and 30. These—especially Figure 29—are probably the most difficult to play, thus making them great warm-up exercises. And you know how much we enjoy warming up. Figure 29 also makes a great diminished arpeggio exercise (in this case, G diminished). It's great for daily exercise, too.

As usual, start very slowly and gradually increase the speed until you can play it with ease at a brighter tempo. I've also included some fingerings that work for me on this particular exercise. You may want to experiment with your own different fingerings.

Now, if you're ever working in Hawaii, Figure 30 will make a handy ending; it's a good exercise, too. Last, but not least, Figure 31 is a TV-jingle-style ending.

These are but a few sample endings. Create your own, and if they're distinctive, you may find people hiring you for your great endings.

By Nathan East

Figure 23.

(Cadence)

Figure 24.

Show

Figure 25.

Swing

Figure 26.

Blues

Figure 27.

Jazz/Swing

Figure 28.

Blues

Figure 29.

Dixieland

Figure 30.

Hawaiian

Figure 31.

Jingle

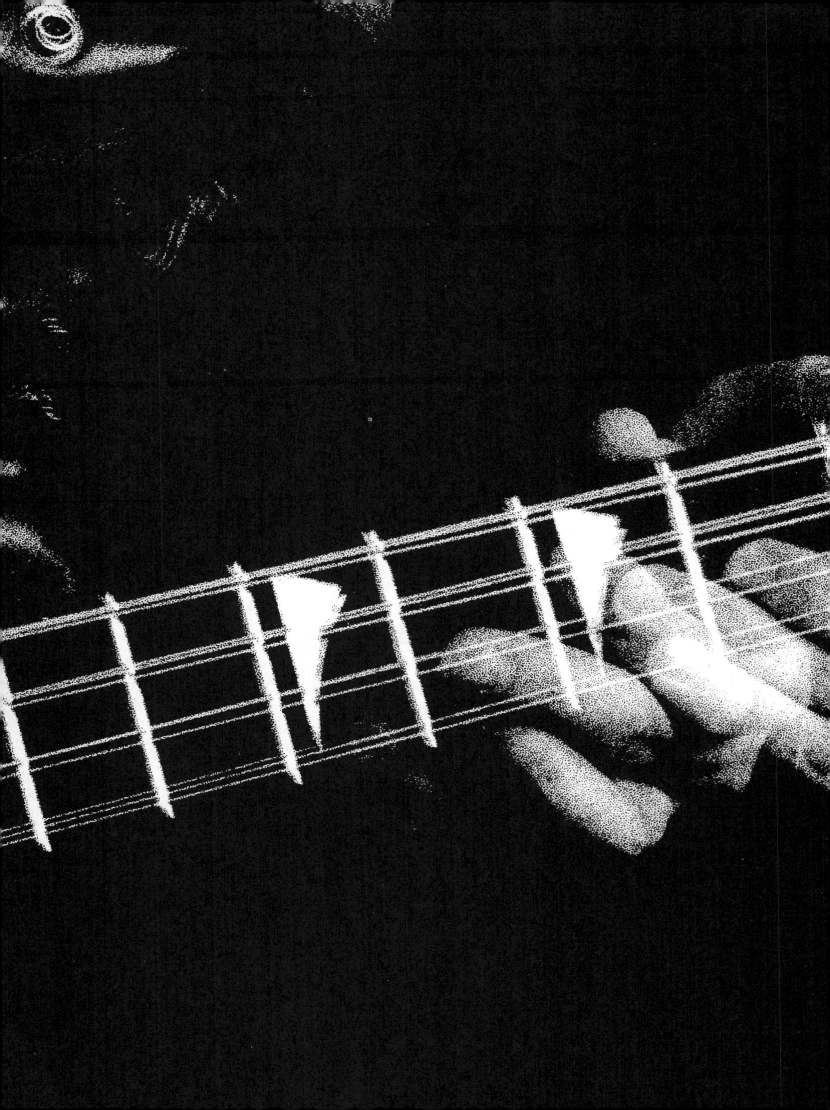

Chapter 7:
Scales

Scales

Types Of Scales

Guitar Player **magazine August 1978**

Sooner or later, almost every bass player will be confronted with a chart that will call for some improvisations within a scale. Usually, it will be indicated like this:

E♭ Dorian

etc.

You will be expected to play an accompanying bass part that outlines the scale (and maintains the scale's feeling or sound). Needless to say, there are many scales to learn. It is even more important to practice them—one at a time—in all 12 keys. Take each one and memorize it, first covering one octave, then two.

At the end of this article is a list of the 15 most commonly used scales. Some of these are modal sequences, which are derived from the major scale. The modes are constructed by starting an eight-note sequence from the various notes in the major scale. Each Roman numeral represents a step of the *C* major scale to start from:

I to I is the *C* Ionian mode
II to II is the *D* Dorian mode
III to III is the *E* Phrygian mode
IV to IV is the *F* Lydian mode
V to V is the *G* Mixolydian mode
VI to VI is the *A* Aeolian mode
VII to VII is the *B* Locrian mode

Here are the various attributes of the scales and modes shown below: The major scale is used with major chords, as well as major 6th and major 7th chords. The Dorian mode is generally applied to minor 7th chords (starting on the root): the Phrygian is used on some minor 7th chords (starting on the root) and on major 7ths (starting on the 3rd). Major 7th and minor 7th chords can be flavored by using the Lydian mode (start your bass line on the root); the Mixolydian is useful on dominant 7th chords (again, start on the root of the chord).

The Aeolian mode (otherwise known as natural minor) can be used with minor and minor 7th chords; you should start on the root. You can use the harmonic minor scale with minor and minor major 7th chords, starting at the root; melodic minor can be used with minor and minor major 7th chords (starting at the root), and dominant 9#11 chords (starting on the 5th). The Locrian mode is applicable to minor 7♭5th, or half-diminished, chords; start this mode on the chord's root. The whole-tone scale can used with augmented 7th chords (starting on the root, 3rd, or 5th). The blues scale can be used on major, minor, minor 7th, and dominant 7th chords; start this scale on the root of the chord.

The major pentatonic scale is generally used with a major, major 6th, or dominant 7th chord, starting from the root. Its counterpart, the minor pentatonic scale, can be used on minor, minor 7th, (starting at the root), and major 6ths chords (starting at the 3rd). The diminished scale may be used with a diminished 7th chord (starting on the root, lowered 3rd, lowered 5th, or double-flatted 7th). It can also be employed with dominant 7♭9 chords (starting on the 3rd, 5th, lowered 7th, or lowered 9th), minor 7♭5th (half-diminished 7th) chords (starting on the root, lowered 3rd, or lowered 5th), and minor 7th chords, starting on the root or lowered 3rd.

By Herb Mickman

Scales And Modes

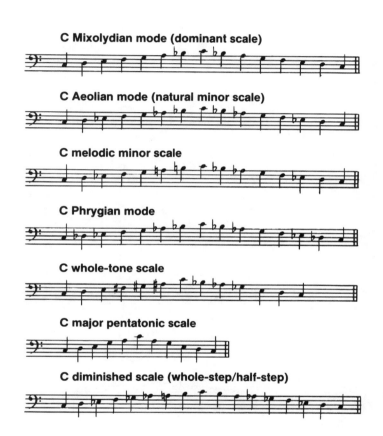

Two-Octave Major Scales

Becoming comfortable with scales everywhere on the fingerboard is necessary for a complete understanding of the bass. We are going up the fingerboard to play six major scales in a two-octave range. First, briefly review the notes that go above the staff. Study Figure 1 below and memorize it.

Guitar Player magazine
August, September 1985

Figure 1.

There are several fingerings for two-octave scales. Memorize the six major scales in Figure 2 with the fingerings indicated. First, take the top fingering and play it every day for at least a week. Then try the scales with the lower fingering, and see which one you like better. Be sure you are aware of every note's name—not just the fingering.

There are a few points to memorize about these scales. All of them start in first position (2nd fret) with the exception of F major, which begins in half position (1st fret, the lowest position on the bass). In all of the scales, your 1st finger will be on the fifth note of the scale in the second octave. Additionally, the 2nd finger will be on the third note in the second octave (with the exception of E major). The sixth note in the second octave of each scale is played with the 4th finger.

In the major keys of G, Ab, and A, the top note is played with the 3rd finger. This pattern starts when you play the note G (on the third ledger line above the staff). This is because the frets start to get closer together, and this fingering compensates for that. (Remember, the 3rd finger doesn't fret notes in the lower registers; it accompanies the 4th finger in holding the string down for better intonation.)

Be sure to follow these concepts: When it says "2nd finger," keep the 1st and 2nd fingers down on the string. When it says "3rd finger," keep the 1st, 2nd, and 3rd fingers down. "4th finger" indicates that all four fingers should be down on the same string. Keep your thumb in the back of the neck, with a big space between your 1st and 2nd fingers, and move your thumb as you change positions.

Figure 2.

On most electric basses, the highest fretted note is E♭, so you will have explored the entire range of the fingerboard. Within these scales, you will find some alternative fingerings. For now, after you have mastered the top fingering, try the fingering below and see which one you like better.

These scales go high and require the use of many ledger lines (Figure 3). One way to omit the ledger lines is to write high notes in the treble clef (Figure 4). But since most bassists don't read treble clef fluently, this isn't very practical. Another way is to stay in bass clef and write notes an octave lower than normal, using the "8va" symbol (short for *octava*), which means to play the notes one octave higher than written (Firgure 5). This is the method I prefer, which makes them easier to read until you've gained experience above the staff.

Figure 3.

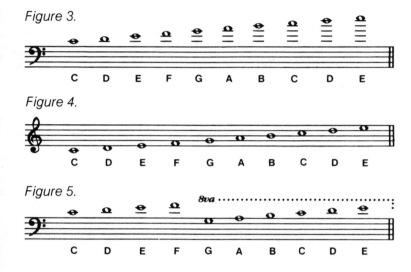

C D E F G A B C D E

Figure 4.

C D E F G A B C D E

Figure 5.

C D E F G A B C D E

Let's look over the scales in Figure 6. These six scales have some similar fingering concepts (they apply to the top fingerings only). In all of these cases, the 1st finger plays the first and fifth notes in the second octave of the scale. Likewise, in the second octave, the 2nd finger plays the third and seventh notes; the 3rd finger holds the sixth and top notes; and the 4th finger frets the second and fourth notes. All start in half or first position (1st and 2nd frets, respectively).

By Herb Mickman

Figure 6.

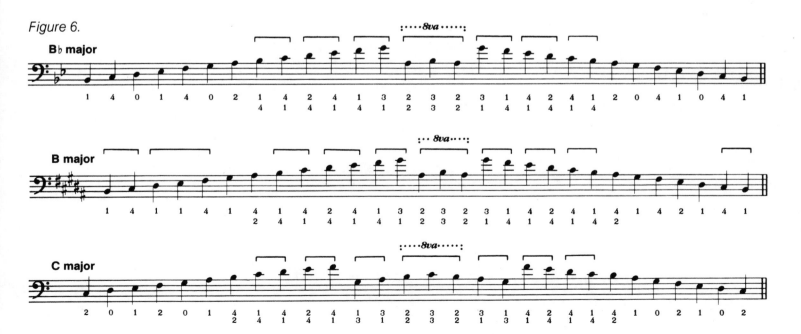

Figure 6 (continued).

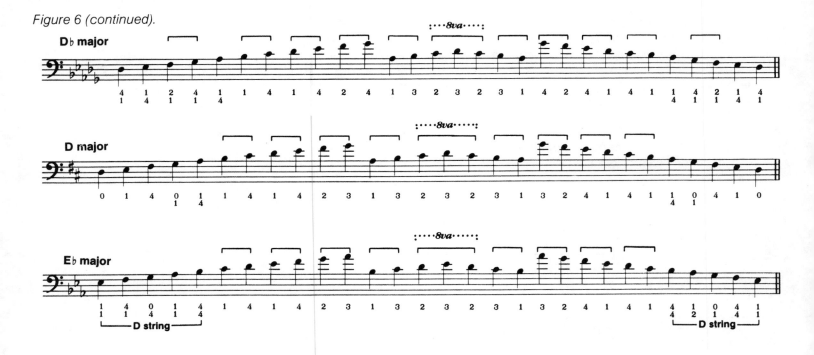

Db major

D major

Eb major

The Natural Minor Scale

***Guitar Player* magazine
February, March 1986

There are three kinds of minor scales: the harmonic minor, the melodic minor, and the natural minor. The following exercises deal with the natural minor scale (also known as the Aeolian mode). If you look at the example below, you can see that compared to the major scale, the natural minor scale has three notes lowered one half-step: the 3rd, 6th, and 7th.

major scale

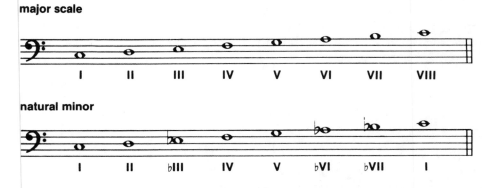

natural minor

Lets take the scales one by one, and try the fingerings that go with them. Watch for position shifts (fingerings in one position are indicated by a bracket *over* a group of notes). As usual, we are using traditional bass positions, so if your index finger is located at the 1st, 2nd, 3rd, 4th, 5th, 6th, 7th, 8th, 9th, 10th, 11th, or 12th fret, the respective positions are: 1/2, I, II, II/III, III, III/IV, IV, V, V/VI, VI, VI/VII, and VII. A bracket *under* a group of notes indicates that the group is to be played on one string.

By Herb Mickman

E minor

E minor

E minor

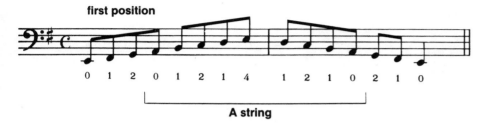

E minor

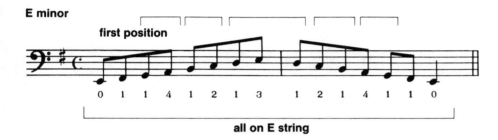

F minor

F minor

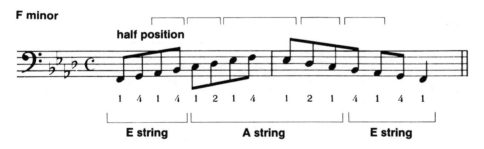

F # minor

F# minor

G minor

half position

4 0 1 4 0 1 4 0　4 1 0 4 1 0 4

G minor

half position

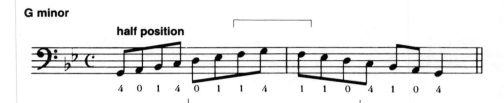

4 0 1 4 0 1 1 4　1 1 0 4 1 0 4

D string

G minor

half position

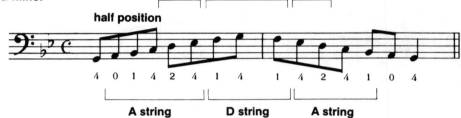

4 0 1 4 2 4 1 4　1 4 2 4 1 0 4

A string **D string** **A string**

B♭ minor

half position

1 2 4 1 2 4 1 4　1 4 2 1 4 2 1

B♭ minor

half position

1 4 1 4 1 2 1 4　1 2 1 4 1 4 1

A string **D string** **A string**

B minor

first position

1 4 0 1 4 0 1 4　1 0 4 1 0 4 1

B minor

first position

1 2 4 1 2 4 1 4　1 4 2 1 4 2 1

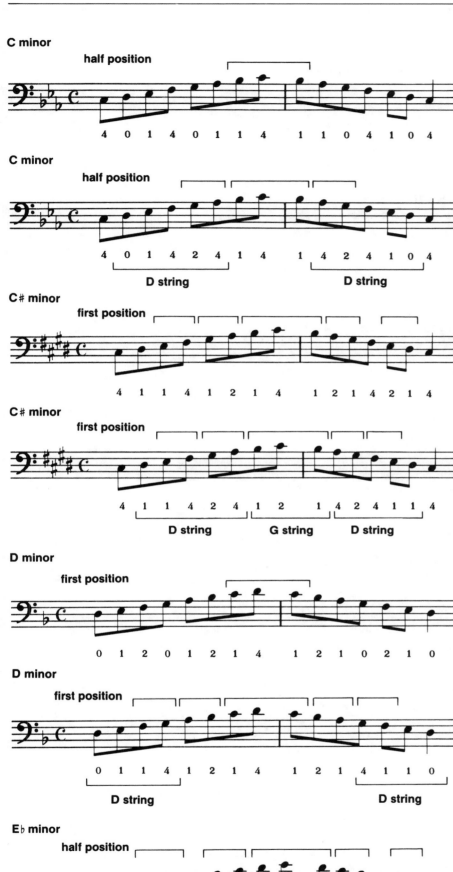

Eb minor

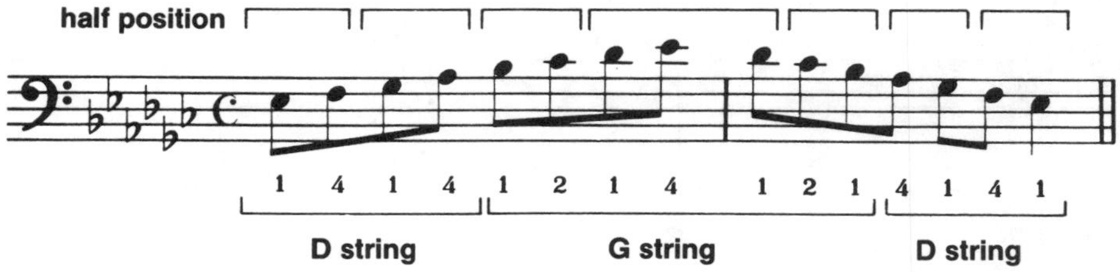

half position

1 4 1 4   1 2 1 4   1 2 1   4 1 4 1

D string   **G string**   **D string**

G# minor

first position

4 1 1 4 1 1 4 1   4 2 1   4 1 1 4

G# minor

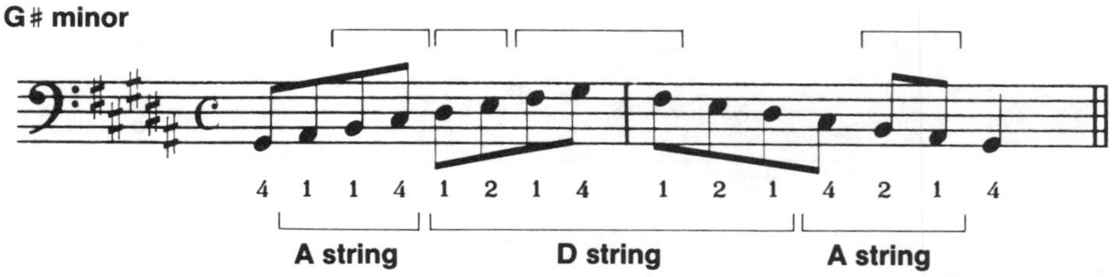

4 1 1 4   1 2 1 4   1 2 1   4 2 1   4

A string   **D string**   **A string**

A minor

half position

0 2 4 0 2 4 0 2   0 4 2 0 4 2 0

A minor

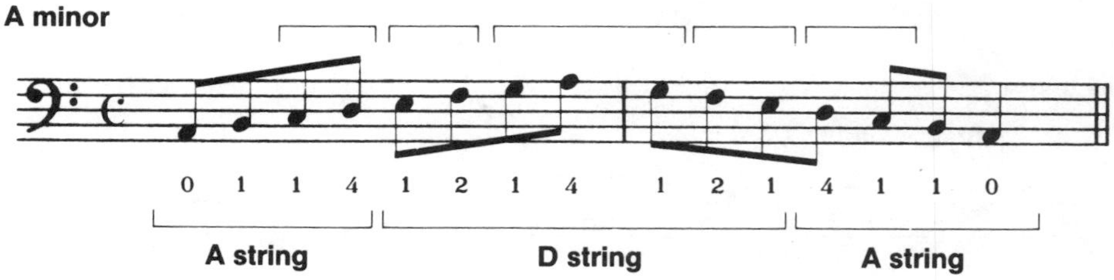

0 1 1 4   1 2 1 4   1 2 1   4 1 1 0

A string   **D string**   **A string**

A minor

0 1 1 4   1 2 1 3   1 2 1   4 1 1 0

all on A string

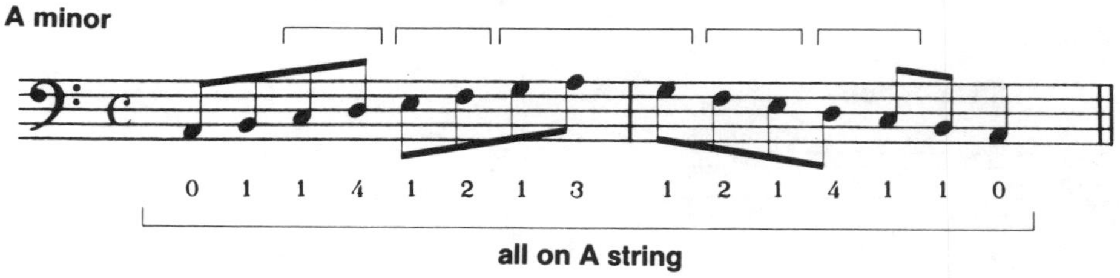

The Diminished Scale

Guitar Player **magazine October 1979**

The first time I heard Ray Brown play bass was at the Newport Jazz Festival, around 1959. I had heard him several times on records, but the impact of hearing this jazz giant in person taught me a valuable lesson. It showed me how helpful it is to see *and* hear a player, rather than just hear him. I was able to pick up quite a few licks that day. The next time he came to town I knew a little bit more about what he was doing, and I managed to copy down what is shown in Figure 7.

Although I didn't get the rhythm accurately, I was able to get this unusual combination of notes and study it. I showed it to a pianist I knew who immediately told me it was a diminished scale. It is formed by alternating intervals of whole-steps and half-steps (see Figure 8). My pianist friend told me that jazz trumpeter Dizzy Gillespie was playing hip patterns on that scale back in 1947!

I was in love with the sound of the scale and began to practice it and construct patterns on it. After a while I could do all the patterns over a two-octave range. Also, my ears began to open up and tell me where to use them. Here are the four chords that the scale works best with and the starting notes for each scale:

Chord Type	Starting Note
Minor 7th	Root or ♭3rd
Half-diminished 7th	Root, ♭3rd or, ♭5th
Diminished 7th	Root, ♭3rd, ♭5th, or ♭♭7th
Dominant 7th ♭9th	3rd, 5th, ♭7th, or ♭9th

Here are several sequences. First master the basic scale (Figure 8). Play it until you have it perfect (one octave in all 12 keys), and then try each sequence in all keys.

Herb Mickman

Figure 7.

Figure 8.

The Minor Pentatonic Scale

***Guitar Player* magazine December 1979**

The use of different types of scales for jazz improvisation goes back to the '40s, when musicians were feeling new influences of such musical giants as saxophonist Charlie Parker, trumpeter Dizzy Gillespie, pianists Bud Powell and Thelonious Monk, and others. Some of the scales that they brought to jazz soloing were the *diminished* and the *whole-tone* scales.

To gain facility with any scale requires a certain amount of practice and experimentation. I believe that doing a lot of musical calisthenics with a scale helps to get your ear used to the various intervals found within it. With enough practice you can sharpen your ear to the point where you are able to follow through on practically any idea you "hear" in your head.

Just running up and down scales in a solo context sounds corny and contrived to an experienced listener, so remember that a scale is just a group of notes that will give a certain sound over the chords utilized in a piece. And although the best improvisers use scales, they will vary them so that they don't sound mechanical.

The minor pentatonic scale (Figure 9) is one of the most common sounds employed in today's music. Just about every great improvisor has used it. And while some have used it consciously, many more play it simply by ear. The minor pentatonic scale can be used along with minor triads, minor 7th chords, and dominant 7th chords, starting on the root of each.

Play each of the patterns below in all 12 keys. Note that Figure 13 has three additional rhythms, which will help break up the monotony of concentrating on scales.

By Herb Mickman

Figure 9.

Figure 10.

Figure 11.

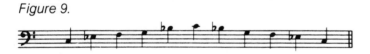

Figure 12.

Figure 13.

Figure 13a.

Figure 13b.

Figure 13c.

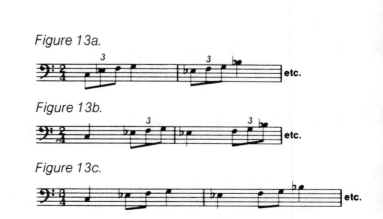

The Whole-Tone Scale

Let's look at what some theorists call a symmetric scale—one that consists of the same interval pattern throughout. We will start with whole-tone intervals (see Figure 14).

The whole-tone scale became popular in jazz improvisation in the late '40s, and some of the jazz licks shown in Figures 15, 16, and 17, were typical of jazz's bebop era. The scale was used with two types of chords: the augmented triad (Figure 18) and the augmented 7th, which is a dominant 7th chord with a raised 5th (Figure 19).

To get the sound of the scale fixed in your ear, you will have to play it over and over many times, until you are certain that you're playing it right. After mastering it over one and then two octaves, start to do the sequences shown in Figures 20, 21, 22, and 23. Play them in all 12 keys. Figure 24 shows how chords can be constructed on each note of the scale; all the triads are augmented. (These chords are the basis for Figures 15 and 25.)

Some of the piano giants who were using this scale were Bud Powell and Thelonious Monk. I would suggest checking out any of their records for some examples of the whole-tone sound. Familiarity with their whole-tone chordal and single-line structures can be a valuable tool for any bassist.

Guitar Player magazine January 1980

By Herb Mickman

Figure 24.

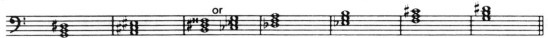

Figure 25.

Encountering The Dorian Mode

***Guitar Player* magazine
January, February 1981**

Many years ago, when I was in high school, I took a harmony course, and through my studies I became aware of different types of scales. One day the teacher told us to place Roman numerals under each note of the major scale. It was explained that if you play all of the notes from I through VIII, or, in other words, I through I (say, *C* to *C*, or *D* to *D*, etc.), the result would be a major scale. There is a Greek name often associated with the major scale: the Ionian mode (see Figure 26).

We found that there were indeed other scales besides the major scale, and proceeding through it until that same note was reached one octave higher, we would be constructing a scale called the Dorian mode (see Figure 27). Whereas the major scale contains half-steps between its 3rd and 4th notes and 7th and 8th notes, the Dorian mode has its half-steps located between the 2nd and 3rd notes and the 6th and 7th notes.

Figure 26.   Figure 27.   Figure 28.

Major scale or Ionian mode   **Dorian mode**   **Gm7**

I   II   III   IV   V   VI   VII   VIII
                                            (I)

The basic concept of how the modes were constructed went in one ear and out the other until a few years later, when I heard a very impressive record called *Kind Of Blue* [Columbia, PC-8163] by trumpeter Miles Davis (with pianist Bill Evans and saxophonists John Coltrane and Cannonball Adderly). Throughout this album, the musicians were involved in improvisations based upon a scale, rather than chords. It turned out to be the Dorian mode that they were working with, and since the '50s this mode has become a standard tool for nearly every jazz musician.

I realized that just knowing the scale's construction wasn't enough to really get it "in my ear," so I began to play the scale over two octaves and in sequences that covered all keys, starting in the lowest positions on the bass, working up.

Before we delve into the Dorian mode exercises below, let me give you a guide to the fingerings I have written under each note:

0 = open string

1 = 1st finger on the string

2 = 1st and 2nd fingers on the string

3 = 1st, 2nd and 3rd fingers on the string

4 = all four fingers on the string

It's important to keep each preceding finger down as you go to the next one; that is, from 1 to 2, from 2 to 3, etc. This helps to improve your tone, plus it makes your motions more efficient. For example, if you must go from the 4th finger to the 1st, you won't have to lift your 4th finger up and put your 1st finger down; rather, you simply lift the 2nd, 3rd, and 4th fingers in one motion, and leave the 1st in place.

Notice that brackets (⌐⌐) are located above some sections of the exercises. All notes under a bracket are to be played in one position; that is, even though you change fingerings, your hand remains poised at the same position.

By Herb Mickman

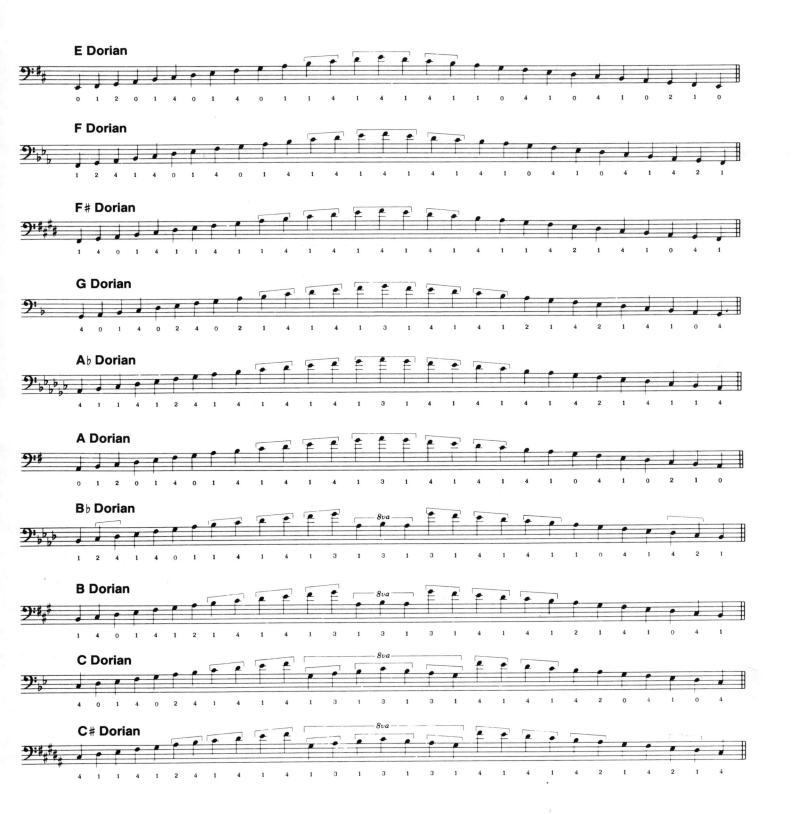

Scales For Dominant 7th Chords

Guitar Player **magazine June 1987**

Let's concentrate on nine scales that are used with a dominant 7th chord (a major triad with a lowered 7th). The first scale, Figure 29, is the Mixolydian mode, which can be built by starting on the fifth note of a major scale and going up an octave. This C Mixolydian mode is the scale for the V chord in the key of F major. Figure 30 is what I call the harmonic minor Mixolydian mode. It's the scale for the V chord in a harmonic minor key (in this case, F harmonic minor).

Figure 31 is built entirely in whole-step intervals, and it can be used with a dominant 7th chord with a raised 5th (also called an augmented 7th chord). Many times an improviser turns a dominant 7th into an augmented 7th chord so that he can play some of the sounds of the scale against it.

Figure 32 is a Mixolydian mode with a raised 11th (or raised 4th). It's often used when the raised 11th is in the melody. Figure 33 is a beautiful scale to use with a dominant 7th with a lowered or raised 9th. It has a specific interval pattern: half-step, whole-step, half-step, whole-step, etc. The scale in Figure 34 has some intervals from the dominant diminished scale and from the whole-tone scale. The scale is built on the 7th step of the melodic minor scale (ascending form), and it's used with the 7#5#9 or 7#5b9.

Figure 35 is a blues scale with a lowered 3rd, a lowered 5th, and a lowered 7th. These are often called blue notes, and they give a particular sound when played over a dominant 7th chord. Figure 36 is a minor pentatonic scale—a first cousin of the blues scale. The difference is that there is a lowered 5th in the blues scale. Our final scale, Figure 37, is a group of notes from the major scales—root, 2, 3, 5, and 6. There are lots of ways to superimpose this over a dominant 7th chord. Many players move up and down major pentatonic chords built on notes other than the chord's root (for example, G♭ major pentatonic over C7).

To really familiarize yourself with these scales, start with the first one and play it up and down over one octave, in all 12 keys, for a week or two. Work through each scale many times without mistakes before going on to the next one. Then try the harmonic minor Mixolydian mode. Don't play any scale over two octaves until you can perform all of these one-octave scales perfectly.

The opportunity to use these scales comes up when we have a chord that lasts for a bar or more. Some of the great improvisers can use them when a chord lasts only one or two beats. A bassist can apply them in both an accompanying context and in a soloing setting. Being aware of the key you're in at a particular place in a song helps you determine which scale to use, and being aware of the melody also indicates which scale to employ.

Here are a few general rules that you might want to follow:

1. Any dominant 7th chord (or augmented 7th chord) is the V chord of a particular key, and that key could be major or minor. Look where it resolves.

2. A lowered 9th in the melody opens up the possibility of using the harmonic minor Mixolydian mode, the dominant diminished scale, or the diminished whole-tone scale.

3. A raised 5th of the chord in the melody opens the door for the whole-tone or diminished whole-tone scale.

If you spend some time practicing these scales, you really get their sounds into your ear, as well as under your fingers.

By Herb Mickman

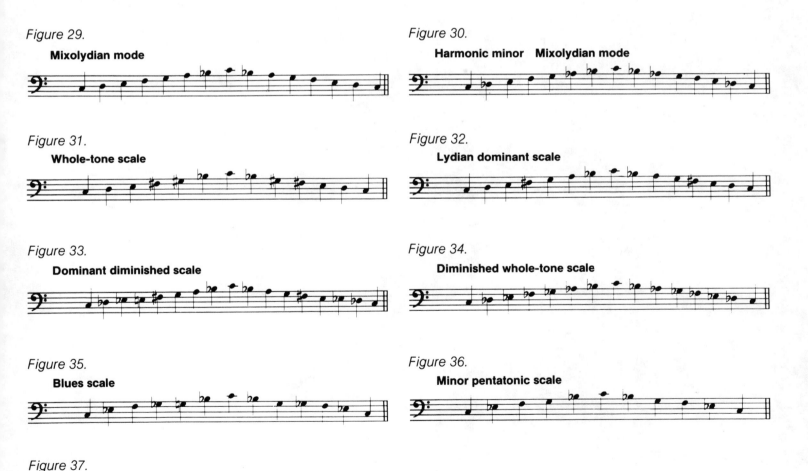

Figure 29.

Mixolydian mode

Figure 30.

Harmonic minor Mixolydian mode

Figure 31.

Whole-tone scale

Figure 32.

Lydian dominant scale

Figure 33.

Dominant diminished scale

Figure 34.

Diminished whole-tone scale

Figure 35.

Blues scale

Figure 36.

Minor pentatonic scale

Figure 37.

Major pentatonic scale

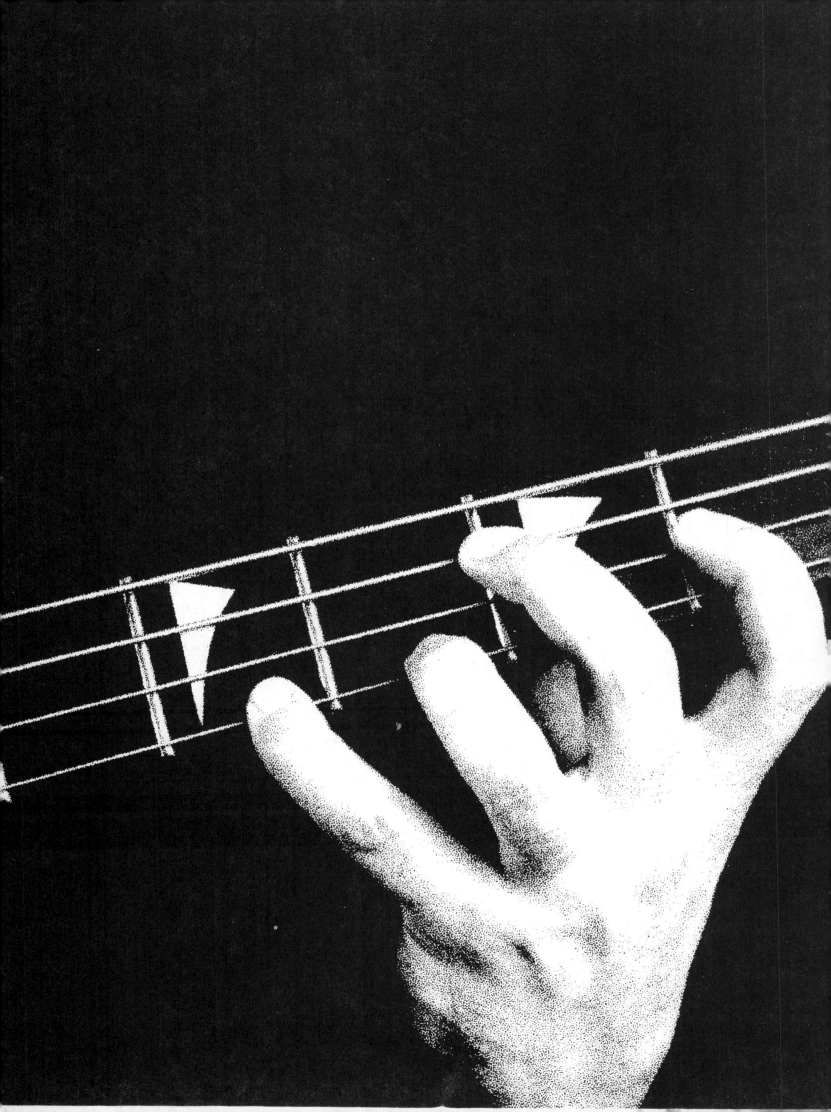

Chapter 8:
Chords

Chords

Chording

Guitar Player magazine
December 1977; January, February 1978

The bass, unlike the piano or guitar, is not known as a chording instrument. However, playing chords on the bass can be practical and enlivening for music when done with sensitivity, creativity, and ability.

Taste, used with integrity, is the most important attribute for playing chords on the bass. If you're in a playing situation where there is an electric piano and a guitar, and a lot of chord progressions instead of rhythm patterns, it's in bad taste for the bass to do the same (unless of course that piece of music is orchestrated so that the bass must chord). If you want to play chords in a situation like this, use them sparsely and intelligently.

* * * *

Thirds and tenths are the same notes, in that raising the third an octave higher than the tonic makes that note a tenth. Every consecutive line and space of the staff, ascending and descending, moves back and forth in major or minor thirds (depending on the scale that is in use).

Figure 1.

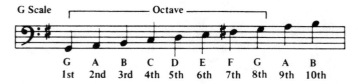

Figure 2.

Major Example (Key of G)

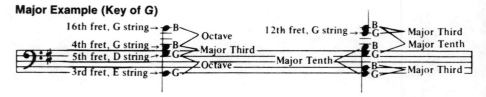

Figure 3.

The key of G minor is related to the key of B♭ and uses that key signature.

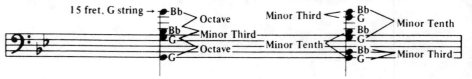

Figure 4 is low in resonance and should be used only to familiarize yourself with thirds. Figure 5 is more practical, because it is an octave higher and will blend more tastefully with other instruments. Figure 6 is the same as 4 and 5, except the spread between notes forms tenths, thereby giving the progressions a good chord sound from the bass.

Figure 4.

Thirds

Figure 5.

Figure 6.

Tenths

Open string chording is more effective in overall sound and performance when the player has the ability to play rhythmically as well as melodically. Let's take a look at the *D* [Figure 7], *A* [Figure 8], and *E* [Figure 9] chord graphs of major and minor thirds and tenths. I've provided some exercises to facilitate the use of a bass line with chords.

Figure 7.

Major Example: Key of *D*

Minor Example: The key of *D* minor is related to *F* major and uses that key signature.

Figure 8.

Major Example: Key of *A*

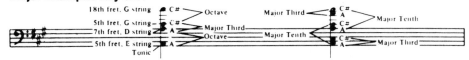

Minor Example: The key of *A* minor is related to *C* major and has no key signature.

The open *E* string is the lowest sounding note on the bass. Therefore, it provides a wide range of workable bass line ideas using the chording technique.

Figure 9.

Major Example: Key of *E*

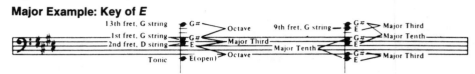

Minor Example: The key of *E* minor is related to *G* major and uses that key signature.

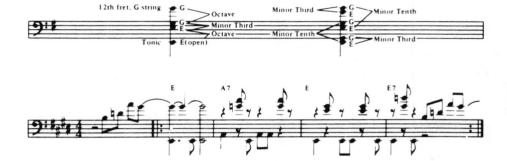

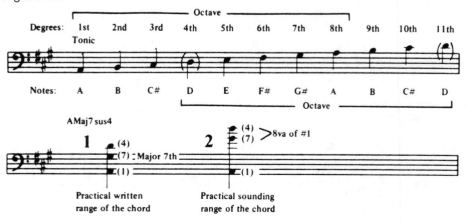

Chording can be heard on the following tunes: Quincy Jones—"Manteca," "Summer In The City," and "First Time," on *You've Got It Bad Girl* [A&M, SP3042]; Lena Horne and Gabor Szabo—"Message To Michael," and "Rocky Raccoon," on *Lena And Gabor* [Skye, SK15]; Len Novey—"Shy Ann." on *No Explanations* [Atco Records, SD33-274]; Donald Byrd—"Love's So Far Away," on *Black Byrd* [Blue Note, KA047-G]; Etta James—"Lay Back Daddy," *Etta James* [Chess, CH 50042].

The chording diagrams, exercises, and bass lines shown here should be used to spur individual changes, resulting in creativity. My concept of creativity in bass lines and patterns involves changing something already played. The notes that comprise our music scale have already been created, and several centuries of popular, ethnic, and categorized music have been written and patterned. The act of *changing something* replaces and represents creativity. Your options are to: 1) musically resist what you don't like; 2) musically solve problems that are personally incorrect; or 3) musically change something to fit your own individual taste. How you resist, solve problems, and/or change musical ideas constitutes your individualism and creativity. Thus, the essence of my theory is that what you *create* musically is only something you've changed.

The suspended chord produces an unresolved sound. Those in Figures 10 and 11 are formed by using the fourth degree of the scale indicated.

Figure 10.

Degrees:	1st	2nd	3rd	4th	5th	6th	7th	8th	9th	10th	11th
	Tonic										
Notes:	A	B	C#	D	E	F#	G#	A	B	C#	D

A Maj7 sus4

Figure 11.

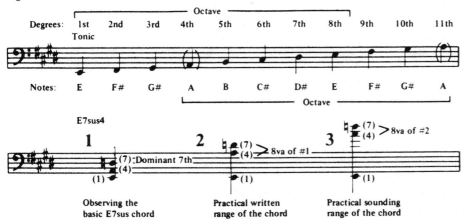

Notice that the eleventh degree of a scale is the same note as the fourth degree. Using either note produces a suspended sound. Your imagination and ability determines which notes you use, and when, how, and where you use them.

"Possessions" is my own composition. It uses major and suspended chords rhythmically to achieve its conception. Below, I've presented a segment of that piece.

By Chuck Rainey

"Possessions"   # By Chuck Rainey

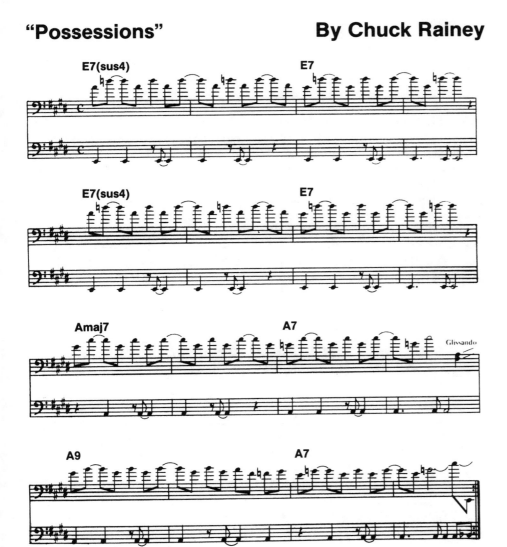

Chords Around The Cycle Of Fifths

Guitar Player **magazine   May 1978**

When I first started to study the string bass at the age of 15, I had a goal in mind: I wanted to be able to play jazz in a group. My first jobs were one-night parties—club dates or casuals. I'll never forget the phone call from a bandleader from another high school, who gave me all the details for my first job and then said, "You can fake, can't you?" I didn't want to blow the gig, so I mumbled, "Sure."

When I got there, the band started to play a lot of standards and popular tunes of the day. There was no rehearsal, and we didn't have chord charts. The leader didn't even tell us the name of the next tune. He held up fingers. For example, three fingers meant three flats, or the key of E♭. Needless to say, I played many more wrong notes than right ones, because my ear wasn't developed, and I didn't know how to memorize bass lines. Later, I played with a pianist a few years older than myself, and he was trying to help me play better bass notes. He frequently would yell out, "Cycle! Follow the cycle!" I had absolutely no idea what he meant. So, he drew this diagram (below) for me and said, "This is the cycle of fifths."

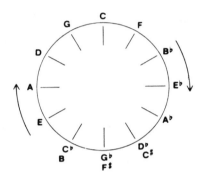

The cycle (or circle) of fifths is a special order that chords move in throughout the course of many songs. Any letter name (*F, C♯,* etc.) can be the perfect fifth note of a key: *C* is the fifth note of *F*; *G* is the fifth note of *C*; etc. Many songs progress in the clockwise pattern I have shown. A great number of theorists and music teachers utilize the pattern in the opposite direction (moving from *C* to *G* to *D*, etc.), but in *practical* usage, the progression that I have shown is more commonly used and therefore more directly helpful to the bassist.

I was told to memorize it, and, as reinforcement, I was introduced to a standard called "All Things You Are" by Jerome Kern. It employs this concept. Figure 12 shows the progression; I've used brackets to mark off each of the chords as they go around the cycle. The song is in *A♭* major but also goes through several other keys.

Figure 12.

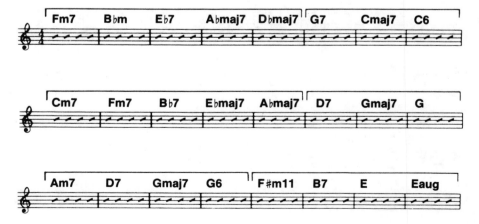

Figure 12 (continued).

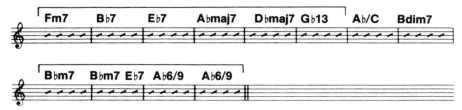

To help you to *really* memorize it, and to be able to recognize a progression based on the cycle of fifths, I've written a few sequences. They should be practiced starting on every note. Play Figure 13 many times, until you have it memorized. Next, start on *F* (on the *D* string). Then begin at *F#, G,* and each note, raised by a half-step, until you can play it starting on any note.

Figure 14, has five sequences involving chords. The patterns in part A follow the root, 3rd, and 5th of every major chord through the cycle. Pattern B is arranged differently: root, 5th, 3rd. Part C combines the two previous patterns, and D incorporates dominant 7th chords. The final section, E, is the reverse of D: You descend though the notes of the dominant 7th chord (root, lowered 7th, 5th, 3rd, and then the root and 3rd of the next chord).

Patterns A, B, and C should eventually be played with minor triads (root, lowered 3rd, 5th), and then diminished (root, lowered 3rd, lowered 5th) and augmented (root, 3rd, raised 5th) triads. Patterns D and E could also be played with the first chord of each measure substituted with a minor 7th chord (lower the 3rd on each dominant 7th chord a half-step; e.g., from *D* to *C#*).

Practice of chords around the cycle of fifths will help expand your knowledge of chord progressions, and really improve your musical ear. Go at it slowly and listen to every note.

By Herb Mickman

Figure 13.

Figure 14a.

Figure 14b.

Figure 14c.

Figure 14d.

Figure 14e.

Chord Substitution

Guitar Player magazine April 1982

Shortly after I began to play my first jobs—mostly parties where we performed dance music—I started working with pianists who would tell me to use specific bass notes in place of the ones I had chosen. Most of the songs we did presented the challenge of deciding upon the correct bass notes by ear—there were no chord charts. I was expected to know all kinds of songs, from old standards to the popular tunes of the day.

When it came to fishing out the right notes, my batting average at age 16 was pretty poor, and I was frustrated. I bought sheet music and fake books, but the challenge of learning a million tunes and providing the best bass notes was mind-boggling. Nevertheless, I was determined to improve myself.

First I knew five songs well, and then ten, and eventually I became intimately involved with hundreds, Just when I thought I had a song covered, though, I would do a gig with a knowledgeable pianist who would say something like, "Play *Db* here instead of *G*."

My obsession with playing the best bass notes prompted me to work at the piano to figure out some alternative bass notes to use with various chords. I discovered a set of common substitutions that are shown below. I hope that the insight these provide helps you to make better decisions on the bandstand.

In my examples, I've given the chords their diatonic number names (numbers that denote the scale tones upon which the chords are built); if this concept is new to you, see Figure 15. In Figure 16, we will cover some variations on the II-V-I chord progression (the chords are actually IIm7-V7-Imaj7).

Figure 15.

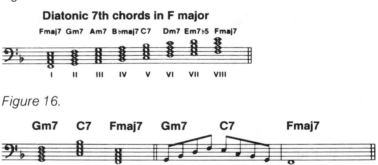

Figure 16.

In Figure 17 there are several common variations on the II-V-I chord progression in the key of *F*. Also, I've written a pattern that should be practiced and memorized in all keys, because its use is called for in so many songs. In other words, an advanced pianist or guitarist may change the original chords to a song in order to improve the flow of the harmony.

A few things determine what variations should be made. One is the melody note and its relationship to the chord (if a note clashes with the chords, it may not be a good choice). Another is the type of song. Some tunes lend themselves to more lush chords, while others sound best with very simple harmony. The key word is *taste*. If a substitution doesn't sound good, don't use it. You'll find that your taste develops from a lot of listening.

The best way to become really aware of chords substitutions is to play a duo or trio gig with a good pianist over a long period of time. There were many opportunities for me during my first years on the bass, and so I had hundreds of impromptu lessons on the bandstand. I also gained a lot of insight by comparing the chords in sheet music to those used on recordings of the same songs.

Practice the following exercises, and try applying their principles to familiar songs. In Figure 17a shows a IIm7b5 acting as a substitute for a IIm7 chord. "b" demonstrates a substitution of a II7 for a IIm7. "c" shows a bVI7, which is a dominant 7th chord raised a b5th from the II chord, as a substitute for the IIm7. "d" illustrates a bII7, which is a dominant 7th chord raised to a b5th from V7, acting as a substitution for the V7. "e" shows a substitution of the V7 with a V7aug. The final example, "f" shows a substitution of the V7 with a VII7, which is a dominant 7th chord in first inversion (its 3rd is in the bass), a minor third higher than the V7 chord.

Once you have practiced these substitutions for a while, you will be able to find many uses for them (try them in songs with which you're already familiar).

By Herb Mickman

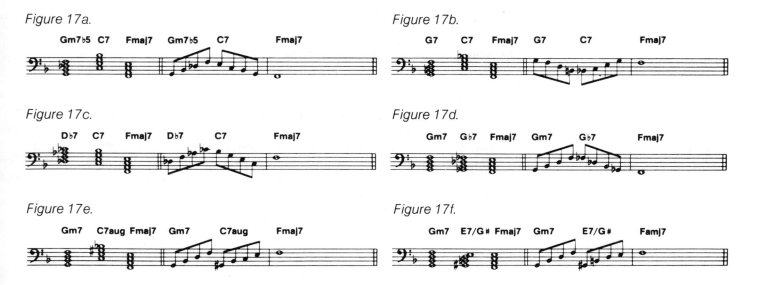

Figure 17a.

Figure 17b.

Figure 17c.

Figure 17d.

Figure 17e.

Figure 17f.

Four-Note Chords

Some of the problems that bass players encounter in learning how to use chords stem from the fact that the overwhelming majority of the examples shown in literature dealing with harmony are written in the treble clef. This is fine for most musicians—violinists, pianists, and, of course, guitarists—but bass players read *bass* clef. Also contributing to the problems confronting the bassist is that reading materials that discuss the nomenclature of chords usually deal only with basic chords, and while many books

Guitar Player **magazine February 1978**

Figure 18.

Chord	Possible notations	Characteristics	Chord	Possible notations	Characteristics
Major 7th	Fmaj7 FM7 F△	A major triad with the 7th step of the major scale added.	Major 6th	F 6	A major triad with the sixth note of the major scale added.
Dominant 7th	F7	A major triad with a lowered 7th added. This chord is often referred to as a 7th chord.	Minor 6th	Fm6 Fmin6 F-6	A minor triad with the sixth note of the major scale added.
Minor 7th	Fm7 Fmin7 Fmi7 F-7	A minor triad with a lowered 7th (dominant 7th with a lowered 3rd).	Augmented 7th	F7#5 Faug7 F7aug5 F+7 F7+5	A dominant 7th with an augmented (raised) 5th, or an augmented triad with a lowered 7th.
Half-diminished 7th	Fm7b5 Fmi7-5 F-7-5 F♯7	This is a minor 7th chord with a lowered (or diminished) 5th.	Minor-major 7th	Fm(maj7) Fmi(add7) Fmin.#7 Fmi-M7 Fmi+7	A minor triad with the seventh note of the major scale added.
Diminished 7th	Fdim7 F°7	A diminished triad with a double-flatted 7th added. This chord can also be thought of as a series of three minor 3rds.	Dominant 7th- suspended 4th	F7sus4 F7sus	A dominant 7th with the fourth note of the major scale replacing the 3rd.

discuss chord construction, very few concern themselves with the specific needs of individual instruments.

So, because of these shortcomings in instructional materials, most bassists pick up what they need to know about the functional aspects of chord construction, usage, etc. from other players at rehearsals, jam sessions, or just in the course of conversation. This isn't necessarily bad, but chord construction is not always the easiest thing to learn, and picking up the "hows" without knowing the "whys" of chord usage can tend to make things more difficult. Also, some important points can be overlooked if the person showing you how to play something only refers to a specific instance and does not give you an idea of general principles that will work in all cases.

Because of these problems, I have put together some guidelines to add to your understanding of chords—their characteristics and notation. It will certainly require a lot of concentration and a concerned effort to memorize and to be able to use these chords as a basis for understanding chordal harmony. It will also take much practice; reading these guidelines will only account for about one percent of what is needed to use chords fluently. It is necessary to write out each of the chords in all 12 keys, and to practice running up and down every one of these examples. As you will see in Figure 18, there may be a few different ways to notate each type of chord; some musicians will use one notation, while others are more inclined to use another. Therefore, it is advisable to familiarize yourself with all of them.

By Herb Mickman

Inversions And Arpeggios

Guitar Player **magazine June 1979**

In the last ten years, chord notations that indicate specific bass notes (other than the root) have become very common. For example, the symbol used to indicate a *B♭m* chord with an *F* bass note looks like this:

B♭m/F

First you see the chord name, followed by the slash, then the bass note. Figure 19 is a bass chord chart to a song with a lot of different chord inversions. Actually, inversions are just rearrangements of the chord notes in such a way that one of the notes other than the root is on the bottom.

Figure 19.

In Figure 20 an *A* major chord is shown in "root position"; that is, with the root on the bottom. Then the chord is stacked in what is known as its "first inversion"—the 3rd is on the bottom. The next part of Figure 20 shows the *A* chord inverted again, this time with the *E* (the 5th of the chord) on the bottom. This is known as the "second inversion."

Figure 20.

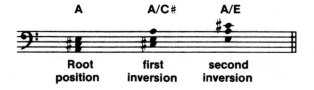

The basic idea behind inversions is not hard to understand, and gaining facility in their use in solos will come about through practice. Below are some routines for just this purpose. Play each one in every key. For example, play the arpeggio in Figure 21 in all 12 keys, using major and minor triads. Then try using diminished and augmented triads. Next, practice Figures 22 and 23 in the same way. The pattern in Figure 24 combines a root-position triad in alternation with a first-inversion triad. After you have mastered Figure 24 (and are able to start on any note), try playing through it by making the first chord of each measure a minor triad—just lower the second note of each bar by one half-step.

By Herb Mickman

Figure 21.

arpeggio

Figure 22.

inversions arpeggiated

Figure 23.

variation with triplets

Figure 24.

variation using circle of fifths

Diminished Chords

There is a skill that almost all bass players will be called upon to use sooner or later: chord chart reading. I'm sure that most of you have had a piece of paper set in front of you with no musical notation other than the abbreviated names of multi-note groupings, otherwise known as chords.

One of the things that I became aware of in my early jam session days was that many chords are not played exactly as written. It seemed that the better guitarists and piano players had some mysterious, magical insight into what the composer actually meant, but was unable to put down on paper. I would like to focus on what I have learned about diminished chords, both as *triads* (see Figure 25) and as four-note chords (see Figure 27).

A diminished triad is a three-note chord that can be explained in two ways. First, it is like a major triad (which includes the root, third, and fifth of a major scale), except with a lowered 3rd and a lowered 5th. A second way to look at it is as a chord composed of two minor third intervals placed one on top of the other (see Figure 26).

A diminished 7th is a four-note chord that has a root, lowered 3rd, lowered 5th, and a double-lowered 7th (see Figure 27). Therefore, a diminished 7th chord is made up of three minor third intervals stacked upon each other(see Figure 28).

I have written a series of exercises to attune your ear to the sound of diminished chords. Be sure to play them in all 12 keys. Note that in these exercises, all 3rds, 5ths, and 7ths are lowered. The pattern in Figure 29 is root, 3rd, 5th, 3rd, root. Figure 30 is just the opposite, following a sequence of 5th, 3rd, root, 3rd, 5th. Figure 31 shows movement

Guitar Player **magazine**
November, December 1980

from the root to the 3rd and 5th, with the process reversed for its descent.

In Figure 33 the first triad ascends and the second one descends. It is a combination of Figures 30 and 31. The arpeggios in Figure 34 run up and down the diminished 7th chord following a pattern of root, 3rd, 5th, 7th, 5th, 3rd, root. Figure 35 flows in the reverse order of Figure 34: 7th, 5th, 3rd, root, 3rd, 5th, 7th. The final example is a combination of the two previous ones; the first arpeggiated chord ascends, the second one descends.

Figure 25. dim. triad Figure 26. minor 3rd Figure 27. dim. 7th Figure 28. minor 3rd

Figure 29.

Figure 30.

Figure 31.

Figure 32.

Figure 33.

Figure 34.

Figure 35.

Figure 36.

Figure 37.

Adim7   Cdim7   E♭dim7   G♭dim7

When I was first learning about chords and their construction I heard someone say that there were only three diminished 7th chords. I couldn't really understand what that meant, since I knew that there were 12 keys. What I didn't realize though, was that each time you play an inversion of a diminished 7th chord you get a combination of notes (built in minor third intervals) that forms *another* diminished 7th chord in root position (see Figure 37).

These chords form three groups which we will call I, II, and III. Because the diminished 7th chords in each group are interchangeable, they can be subsituted for each other (see Figure 38).

If you take the top three notes of a dominant 7th chord and add a lowered 9th, you will find a diminished 7th chord (see Figure 39).

The E diminished 7th is part of group II. Sometimes when the chord would be better written as C7b9, the composer will only notate a part of it—the Edim7 (or Gdim7 or Bbdim7).

In a diminished 7th chord, the intervals separating successive notes are equal; these intervals are minor thirds. As a result, each diminished 7th can perform several functions depending on which tone serves as the root. For example, the Edim7 contains the same notes as a Gdim7, Bbdim7 (A#dim7), and C#dim7 (Dbdim7). Thus, a single group of notes—in this case, Edim7—can effectively provide several chords, and all of them could be used as weak substitutes for the C7b9.

Choosing the best inversion depends on where the diminished 7th is headed. Usually it leads to a minor triad or a minor 7th chord. Suppose it is leading to Fm7. In the circle of 5ths, C leads to F. Therefore, a C7 chord leads to an F chord. A C7 also leads to Fm or Fm7. Many times, when a dominant 7th leads to a minor chord, that dominant 7th will have a lowered 9th. So it is common to see a weak diminished 7th lead to the Fm7 (instead of C7b9).

To help you become familiar with the sound of this progression, I've included a group of melodic exercises to be played in all 12 keys (Figure 40). You will also want to refer to the section on scales to check out the patterns based on the diminished scale.

The first chord is Dm. The second is either Gdim7, Bbdim7, C#dim7, or Edim7. The second chord is really an A7b9. That's the way the experienced pianist or guitarist would think of it. The A7bb9 is the V chord in the key of D minor, and it progresses to the Dm chord naturally.

By Herb Mickman

Figure 38.

Group I

Cdim7 (B#dim7) = Ebdim7(D#dim7) = Gbdim7 (F#dim7) = Adim7

Group II

C#dim7(Dbdim7)= Edim 7 (Fbdim 7) = Gdim7 = Bbdim7 (A#dim7)

Group III

Ddim7 = Fdim7 (E#dim7) = Abdim7 (G#dim7)= Cbdim7 (Bdim7)

Figure 39.

C7   C7b9   Edim7

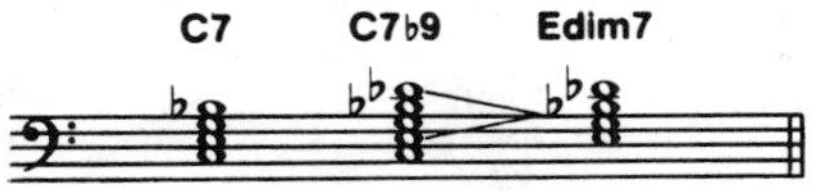

Figure 40.

Patterns with minor and diminished chords:

An Introduction To The Minor 7th Chord

Guitar Player magazine October 1981

Below is an explanation of how the minor 7th chord comes about. First you see an *Fmaj* triad. Then the 7th note of the major scale is added on top, forming a "major 7th" chord. If you lower the 7th note by a half-step you then get a *dominant 7th* chord; in this case it's known as the *F7*. If you lower the 3rd of the dominant 7th chord, you now have a *minor 7th* chord.

Looking at the three bottom notes of a minor 7th you see a minor triad. The interval between the bottom note and the top note is a minor 7th. These are the ingredients that make up this very common chord. If this is new to you, I would suggest writing out all 12 minor 7th chords, so that you can see the notes in front of you.

Figure 42 goes up and down each chord in this manner: root, ♭3rd, 5th, ♭7th, 5th, ♭3rd, and root. Start on the low *Emin7* chord and go up chromatically to the next *Emin7* chord; then come back down. Figure 43 simply follows a format of root, ♭3rd, 5th, and ♭7th on the way up, and ♭7th, 5th, ♭3rd, and root on the way down. Figure 44 is just the reverse of Figure 43 starting on ♭7th, 5th, ♭3rd, and root. Figure 45 combines Figures 43 and 44: One minor 7th goes up and the one that's a half-step higher comes down.

There is a lot of work on this page, so don't expect to play all the exercises perfectly in one afternoon. Work on Figure 42 for one or two weeks until you can go through it evenly and in tempo. Then spend a few weeks on Figures 43, 44, and 45. The ultimate goal is to be able to play Figure 45 starting on any note—going up and down one octave. You'll not only learn the chords, but you'll learn some more of the fingerboard.

By Herb Mickman

Figure 41.

Figure 42.

Figure 43.

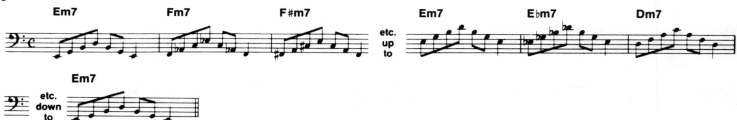

Figure 44.

Figure 45.

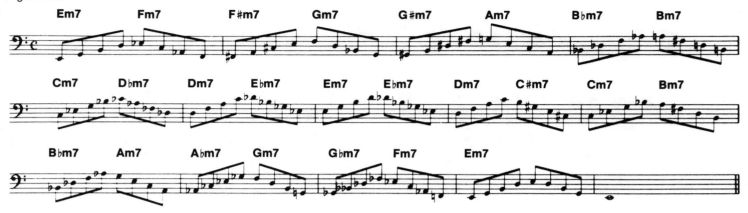

The Half-Diminished 7th Chord

My introduction to chords came with a series of piano lessons dealing with popular music. I was 11 years old, and quite reluctant to get into any serious practice, and the teacher only gave me chords I would need—the chords in the songs—and nothing more. I remember trying to play by ear, and how horrible I was because I didn't know what I was doing.

A few years later, I took a harmony course in high school, which really helped me understand the various chords and their construction. One day I was introduced to a minor 7th chord with a lowered (flatted) 5th; see Figure 46. The common name for this type of chord (which features a ♭3, ♭5, and ♭7) is the *half-diminished 7th*.

Here is a series of exercises to practice in order to familiarize yourself with its construction. Practice Figure 47 slowly up and down over one octave until you can play it from memory, evenly and in tempo. Next, work on Figure 48 in the same manner, and then progress to Figure 49. This final example should eventually be worked out starting on any note, ascending and descending in tempo.

Try to play these patterns with the least amount of shifts (movements from one hand position to another). If you play the ♭5 and ♭7 of each chord within one position, you will be able to accomplish this. When practicing each pattern, be sure you're thinking of the full name of the chord and that you know every note that you're playing.

Guitar Player **magazine**
November, December 1981

Figure 46.

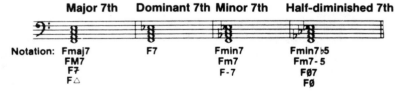

Figure 47.

Figure 48.

Figure 49.

Figure 50. Diatonic 7th chords in F major:

Figure 51.

Figure 52.

Figure 53.

Figure 54.

Figure 55.

Figure 56.

Figure 57.

Figure 58.

Figure 59.

Those of you who are familiar with the diatonic 7th chords (see Figure 50) will know that the II chord of any major key is a minor 7th chord. A very common chord progression consists of the II chord going to the V (see Figure 51). A half-diminished 7th chord built on the second step of the major scale can be used as a substitute for the normal II chord, which is a minor 7th (see Figure 52). This substitution works best when the melody note of the minor 7th is the root, lowered 3rd, or lowered 7th of the chord. However, the key word here is *taste*. Figure 53 illustrates the use of half-diminished 7th chords in a chord progression based on the cycle of 5ths, starting with the *Bm7b5* chord in the key of *F*.

I really became aware of how often this chord is used as a substitute for the minor 7th chord when I started listening to some of the great jazz pianists. I would hear them play a song that I thought I knew, and became aware of how often they lowered the 5th of the minor 7th chords. I've heard many jazz bass players use lines like the ones shown in Figures 54 and 55. These bass lines should be practiced and memorized in all 12 keys.

Another important thing I discovered by listening to great jazz pianists was how a minor 6th chord was really a half-diminished 7th chord in an inversion. Look at Figure 56, and see how the inversions of an *Fm6* work. The third inversion is actually a *Dm7b5* in root position. The bass player should use a *D* note to hold down this chord.

A very common progression that you'll run across in sheet music is a *Fm6* to *G7*. I noticed that the more knowledgeable pianists and bassists would play a *Dm7♭5* to a *G7* in that situation (see Figure 57). The *D* to *G* root movement is also found in the cycle of fifths. Figure 58 shows a typical chord progression, and then shows how half-diminished 7th chords are substituted for the minor 6ths.

If you look back at Figure 50, you will see that the VII chord of any major key is a half-diminished 7th. This VII chord functions like a II chord of another key. For example, *E* is the second note of what key? The answer is *D*. So, *Em7♭5* is the II half-diminished 7th chord in the key of *D*. Remember about II chords going to V chords? For instance, the V chord in the key of *D* is *A7*—the V chord of *D*. The key of *D* at this point could be either *D* major or *D* minor. Figure 59 is a typical chord progression showing how the *E* half-diminished chord works in the key of *F*. It's the II of *D* minor.

By Herb Mickman

Understanding Major 6th Chords

Here are some ways to practice four-note chords called major 6ths. If you look at Figure 60, you'll see a major triad with a major 6th (the sixth note of the major scale). It is that combination of the major triad and the major 6th that forms a major 6th chord. It is often just called a 6th chord—you must assume it is major. To the right of the major 6th chord shown in Figure 61 is the minor 6th. It has a triad with a lowered (or minor) 3rd, and then a major 6th is added on top. Remember: You will gain more improvisational fluency if you have the sounds of these chords in your ear and under your fingers.

Figure 61 shows various ways to practice the major 6th chords. Figure 61a has each one going up chromatically from the root through the 6th. Then the pattern descends, starting with the 6th of each chord. Figure 61b is just the reverse: It ascends chromatically, starting on the the 6th of each chord, and comes down from each chord's root. Figure 61c mixes the concepts of a and b. One major 6th goes up, and the chord that's a half-step higher goes down (from its 6th to its root).

Spend a good week on 61a until it's memorized; then try it from *F* to *F, F♯* to *F♯*, etc. Practice 61a, b, and c evenly in tempo.

By Herb Mickman

Guitar Player **magazine December 1983**

Figure 60.

Figure 61a.

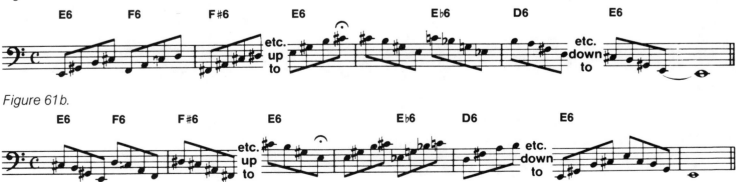

Figure 61b.

Figure 61c.

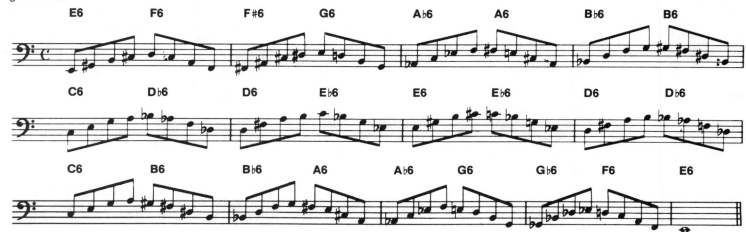

Understanding 9th Chords

Guitar Player **magazine**
September, October 1983

I've illustrated ways to practice three-and four-note chords; now I'd like to explain *five*-note (9th) chords. I hope to clear up some cobwebs.

Figure 62 shows a major scale and the location of the 9th—it's really the second note of the scale, but an octave higher. The 9th is one of the most common tones used to color a chord (make it sound richer), so we should become thoroughly acquainted with it. As shown in Figure 62, the 9ths used with chords can be either major, lowered (major minus one half-step), or raised (a half-step larger than major).

Figure 63 shows how the 9th may be added to various four-note chords. The chords shown are only used to illustrate construction of 9th harmonies—they are not generally played in this register or with these voicings on the piano. I've put them down in the bass clef so you can see how all the various chords would be built over one root (*C*, in this case). Notice that in Figure 63, only the major 9th is added to the four-note chords.

In Figure 64 we see that both the dominant 7th and augmented 7th (a dominant 7th chord with a raised 5th) may have either a major, lowered, or raised 9th degree added on. Many times the exact type of 9th added to the basic 7th chord structure will be determined by the melody of the song; the 9th is often a melody note.

Study suggestions: Carefully analyze the chord constructions shown here; get to know their intervallic structure. Then take one type of 9th chord at a time and write it out in all 12 keys—in pencil and away from your bass. Follow the order of Figure 65, where you'll also find the various ways these five-note chords are written in lead sheet shorthand.

By Herb Mickman

Figure 62.

Figure 63.

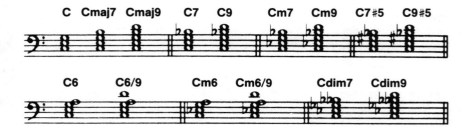

Figure 64.

Figure 65.

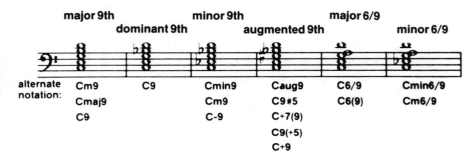

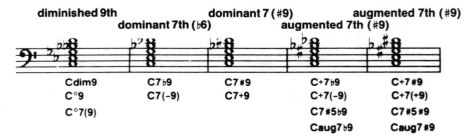

Understanding 11th And 13th Chords

About a year-and-a-half after I started playing the string bass, I began rehearsals with a 16-piece jazz band. The bass parts were about 70% chord reading and 30% notes (to be played exactly as written). I had some chord knowledge before starting on bass from several years of piano lessons, and I was familiar with most types of four-note chords (see Figure 66).

However, when I saw symbols for 11th and 13th chords, I was not able to quickly figure them out. I decided to reduce all 11ths and 13ths down to 7th chords. My responsibility as a bassist was to play the roots on downbeats and a walking bass line with an even pulse. I learned a lot by reading the chord symbols.

Later on, I started to feel the limitations of my chord understanding. I began asking knowledgeable pianists a lot of questions about chords and did a lot of research. A year or so later I was able to expand my knowledge considerably by taking a few intense

Guitar Player **magazine February 1984**

lessons with the late jazz bassist Charles Mingus. He opened a big door by showing me what to practice in order to expand my understanding of chords all over the fingerboard.

As I worked with more advanced players, I began to find out how certain chords I had learned in theory books were not constructed the same way in the contemporary music world. I'd like to explain why. Notice that the examples show the notes in the chord. They are not meant to be played together..

Before you tackle any five-, six-, or seven-note chords, it is absolutely imperative that you have a thorough understanding of four-note chords. Study all the chords in Figure 66, noting their construction. Figure 67 shows the various kinds of 9th chords. Figure 68 demonstrates how we can build a four-note chord from a triad by adding the major 7th (in this case, *E*). If we add the 9th (*G*) to the *Fmaj7*, it becomes an *Fmaj9*.

Figure 69a shows what happens when we add the 11th. This chord is called an 11th in some books, but it is not the 11th chord meant by chord symbols. The chord to its right is an *F11* (Figure 69b). It is a dominant 9th with the added 11th on top. However, this chord is almost never used in this way. In an 11th chord, we omit the 3rd (as it clashes with the 11th on top, since an 11th is essentially a 4th—is only a half-step away from the 3rd).

Figure 69c is a dominant 11th—also known as *F11*. Another way of thinking about a dominant 11th (or just plain 11th) chord is that it is a minor 7th chord that is a fifth higher over the root. In other words *Cm7* over *F* is an *F11*. In Figure 70 we have another contemporary sound—*F#11♭9* or a *C* half-diminished 7th over *F*. Figure 71 shows a very common chord—the minor 11th (a minor 9th with the 11th added on top). Note that the 11ths in Figures 69, 70, and 71 have been the perfect 11th (the fourth note of the scale, one octave higher).

Now in Figure 72 we are going to add the raised 11th (#11) to a dominant 9th. In Figure 72b I show how this sound is really used: We omit the 5th, since we would otherwise have a clash with the top *B* note (the 11th, or ♭5th of the chord). Figure 72c shows the same chord with a lowered 9th (♭9). These are very common jazz sounds.

Figure 73 takes us into the world of 13th chords. Figure 73a is an *Fmaj9*, while Figure 73b shows a chord that is rarely, if ever, used: the major 9th with the 11th on top. Figure 73c is what seems to be a 13th chord. Not really! In the real world, we would omit the 11th from the 13th chord. Figure 73d is a common dominant 13th chord (very commonly called *F13*) Very often the raised 11th is added to the 13th chord for color. Figure 73e shows an *F13* with a raised 11th. Figure 73f is the same *F13* with a lowered 9th and a raised 11th. Figure 73g is a major 13th. It could also be thought of as a *Gmaj* triad over an *Fmaj7* chord.

Now that you've read all this technical information, what can you do to learn it? First, I would say, take each 7th chord in Figure 66 and write it out in all keys—without the aid of a bass. Next, do the same with the 9th chords in Figure 67. Then go through all the 11th chords in Figures 69, 70, 71, and 72. Finally, write out all the 13th chords in Figure 73.

This is only the start. To really know them, you must practice them in all keys up and down the fingerboard. I've covered exercises on triads, 7th chords, and 9th chords previously, so I won't illustrate them here. I hope you've been doing your homework. Figure 74 shows an arpeggio pattern on a 13th chord. The example runs up and down an *F13* chord with a raised 11th. This concept can be applied to all the 11th and 13th chords shown here. Practice these chord types—they're an important part of a good understanding of bass technique. A lot of the so-called far-out improvisation comes from knowing and using the 11th and 13th chords, such as those shown on this page.

By Herb Mickman

Figure 66.

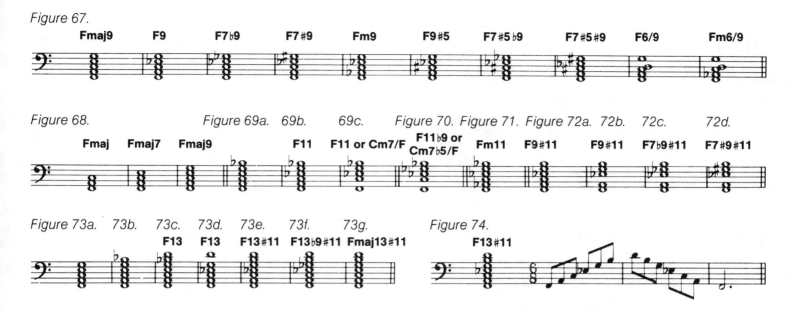

Figure 67.

Figure 68.   Figure 69a. 69b.   69c.   Figure 70. Figure 71. Figure 72a. 72b.   72c.   72d.

Figure 73a. 73b. 73c. 73d. 73e. 73f. 73g.   Figure 74.

Chord-Melody For Bass

For as long as I've been playing bass, I've had a desire to find new and different ideas to apply to my instrument. This desire comes from my natural inquisitiveness when playing music and my great feeling of boredom hearing myself working through the same doo-doo over and over. In order to enlighten myself to the multitudes of possibilities, it became necessary for me to participate in as many musical situations and with as many musicians as I could.

Most notable in my background were associations with Steve Smith, who is now a bandleader in his own right, pianist Gil Goldstein (formerly of drummer Billy Cobham's band; now living in Switzerland), guitarist Mike Stern, formerly with trumpeter Miles Davis, and guitarist Mick Goodrick (formerly with vibraphonist Gary Burton). For over eight years as a professional, I've played with hundreds of the world's best musicians. But I owe my concept of time, melody, attitude, and chord sense to the four musicians named above. Finally, drummer Bill Bruford deserves mention for helping me learn about stage presence, bass tone, and studio techniques (among other things).

Since I am a product of my background and my collective musical input, I feel the desire to do new things on the bass. Keep in mind that although I'm always yakking about nonbass-like playing, the instrument is traditionally supposed to perform a root-note function within the rhythm section. Nothing wrong in this. Neal Stubenhaus, one of the West Coast's premier studio bassists, makes an excellent living by playing the bass the way God and Leo Fender intended. His time is great, his sound is great, and even though he's not playing the bass with a lot of flash and speed, so what?

Below is my arrangement of the old southern tune "Dixie." Being bored with my own playing, I started using chords and counterpoint melodies when working alone, just to pass the time. My chordal sense became strong enough for me to use it when performing with I.O.U., Allan Holdsworth's band. Allan would solo, and I would supply bass notes and chords to fill up a lot of tonal areas, thereby making the group sound larger than an instrumental trio (actually it was a quartet, but the singer, Paul Williams, didn't play an instrument).

My rendition of the piece is in *B* major. Pay attention to the way the sharps, flats, and naturals are used in each bar. You will find some *B*♯s and *E*♯s and one *C* double-sharp (the enharmonic equivalent of *D*) in the arrangement.

Guitar Player **magazine February 1984**

By Jeff Berlin

"Dixie"

Traditional, arr. by Jeff Berlin

**Slowly
Rubato**

Index finger of right hand holds F♯. Strum whole chord with 4th finger of right hand.

Bridge

rit.

Held with index finger of right hand and plucked with right thumb.

Facing page, Jaco Pastorius

Chapter 9:
Bass
Modification

Bass Modification

Rewiring Your Bass

Guitar Player magazine March 1987

In contrast to the "fat," sometimes muddy but punchy tone of the stock Fender Precision Bass, there lies within the circuitry of the instrument a sound that is cleaner and has a bit more "headroom"—a useful alternative in situations where distortion and clipping are not desirable. Adding a switch allows the choice of a fat, punchy texture for live performance, or a more defined tone for recording. Armed with a few basic facts, a soldering iron, and the included wiring diagram, you can have this alternate tone at your fingertips whenever you need it.

First, the facts: The Precision Bass has a humbucking pickup. It is similar in some ways to the humbucker found, for instance, on a Gibson Les Paul Standard. There are two coils that are magnetically opposed and wired out of phase, which results in a sound that is "in phase," but with any extraneous hum cancelled. The P-Bass pickup also has series-lined coils like a guitar pickup. It differs from a guitar pickup, though, in that each coil doesn't sense all of the strings. Each coil of a Precision's pickup is actually only a *half-coil*, sensing just two of the four strings. This allows it to have a narrow magnetic aperture, more like a single-coil pickup. Fender also employed this split pickup design on the Mustang bass and Electric XII 12-string. (We may contrast this design to the Gibson bass humbucking design used on the EB-O and other basses, which has full-width coils, a wide magnetic aperture, and a *really* muddy sound.)

With a throw of a switch, our suggested rewiring changes the series-linked coils to parallel-linked coils. Electrically, this results in an impedance change. Using a volt-ohm meter to measure the DC resistance, we find that the parallel-linked mode gives us one-quarter of the resistance of the series-linked mode. This resistance reading is a round indicator of the change in impedance. What this means to our ears is that with the pickups in the parallel mode, we will experience a bit less output, but will also gain a smoother response over a wider frequency range. The series mode has greater output, but it sacrifices top-end definition, and although it has a punchier attack, the attack may be perceived as "rounder." (Note that this change is more dramatic with the higher-output pickups offered as replacements or found stock in some Precision-style models. The stock Precision pickup has a DC resistance of about 11k ohms.)

For this modification, I recommend using a push-pull type of switch mounted on a 250k ohm audio-taper potentiometer. These are often called push-pull pots, and are made by a variety of manufacturers. Your local music store should be able to help you obtain one. The switch must be the DPDT (double-pole/double-throw) type. Using this push-pull pot allows you to make this modification without drilling or routing your bass, thereby maintaining its original appearance. If you prefer a separate switch, a mini DPDT toggle can be mounted between the volume and tone pots, or between the tone pot and jack, but you must drill a 1/4" hole in your pickguard. No wood will need to be removed.

A word of caution: Before carrying out this project, please assess your skills carefully. It's no fun to have your bass wired and ready to play when your fingers are burned. If you attempt the modification, wear safety glasses and use rosin-core solder *only*. Never use acid-core solder for any electronic project. Also, if you aren't up to the job, ask an electronics-oriented friend, or take your bass to a repairman.

Removing the pickguard, controls, and pickup from your bass is easy. Referring to the diagram labeled "Stock," note the wire that connects the two coils to each other. Find this wire on your pickup. It must be cut in half and stripped; then additional wire that is long enough to reach back to the control cavity must be spliced to each half. Insulate these splices with shrink-wrap tubing or a bit of electrical tape. I do not recommend that these wires be removed from the pickup terminals, as this requires specialized knowledge to avoid damaging the pickup. Splicing is strongly recommended here. I also don't recommend removing the plastic cover from the pickup coils, since this may expose the fine wires to potential damage.

Follow the diagram carefully and proceed slowly. Before beginning the project, be sure that you compare the two diagrams and that you understand the changes. Note that except for replacing the standard tone pot with the switchable one, the only changes to the stock wiring involve the linking wire between the coils. Avoid overheating the switch terminals, and be sure that the soldered joints are secure; this will avoid problems and disappointment later.

By Ralph Novak

Figure 1.

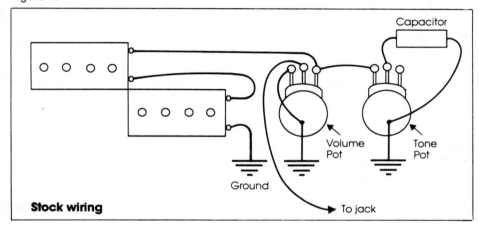

Stock wiring

Figure 2.

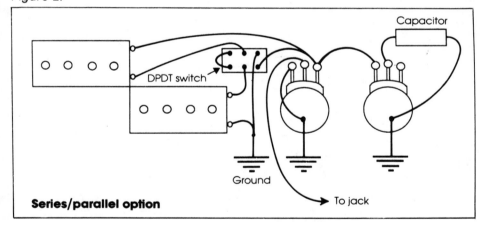

Series/parallel option

Doctoring Your Jazz Bass For More Sounds

Many modifications for guitars and basses require drilling and other alterations to the physical appearance of the instruments, and while they often provide new sonic options, they sometimes make it impossible to get the original sound. Here's a simple do-it-your-self project for Fender Jazz Bass owners—and owners of the many Jazz Bass copies—that expands the tonal capabilities of the instrument, while retaining the original sounds and appearance.

The principle employed here is varying the impedance of the combined pickups, in order to alter the tone. The usual *parallel* combination provides the classic clean, clear tone with lots of top end that we expect from a Jazz Bass. Flipping the switch combines these same pickups *in series*, yielding a tone with a fatter midrange—a rounder edge—and a bit more output. So, you get a sort of Fender Precision Bass tone, but your bass still retains its Jazz Bass character.

To rewire your bass for these added tones, you need basic soldering skills and tools

Guitar Player **magazine April 1986**

and a 250k audio-taper pot (potentiometer) with a built-in DPDT (double-pole/double-throw) push/pull switch. There are several brands of these push/pull pots available in music stores; try to get one with a solid shaft to accommodate the set-screw in the Jazz Bass' stock knob. **Caution:** If you don't have much soldering or rewiring experience, either take your instrument to a pro, or ask for help from a friend who can handle the job.

Series/parallel linking of pickup coils is nothing new. It is common on guitars with humbucking pickups. However, the independent volume control for each coil of the Jazz Bass complicates this usually simple arrangement. I've worked out a wiring system that maintains the individual volume control in both series and parallel modes and uses only the added DPDT switch on the tone pot to accomplish this.

It's noteworthy that stock Jazz Basses have pickups that are magnetically opposite, for hum-cancelling. If you aren't sure that your pickups are stock, or if you have one of the many Jazz Bass copies and want to know if the pickups are magnetically opposite, you can make the determination with a magnet. Bring one pole of the magnet close to one pickup, and then the other pole. One should repel the magnet, while the other should attract it. If this isn't the case, then the pickups are *not* magnetically opposite, your bass is probably noisier than most, and therefore this modification isn't recommended. Likewise, avoid this modification if you have extra-hot pickups or multi-coil (stacked) pickups in your bass, because the combined impedance would be too great to achieve a useful tone in the series mode.

Follow the diagram carefully, and especially note the modification to the bridge-pickup volume pot: The grounded lug must be unsoldered from the metal back of the pot, and then pulled away so that it doesn't unintentionally contact ground. Be neat and go slowly, especially when wiring the DPDT switch.

By Ralph Novak

Figure 3.

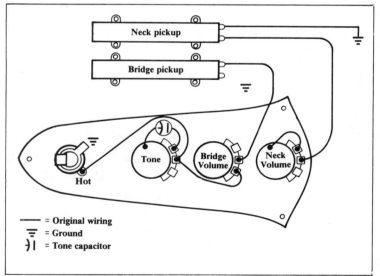

Figure 4.

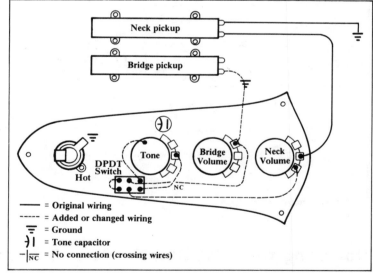

Installing A Master Volume And Pickup Fader

***Guitar Player* magazine June 1987**

The usual configuration of one tone and two volume controls on Fender Jazz Basses and basses with a combination of Jazz- and Precision-style pickups can be easily changed to a master volume, pickup selection fader, and tone setup. Only the stock parts and a few inches of wire are needed.

Before-and-after schematic drawings show how to make the modification. Solder carefully. If you aren't adept at soldering or rewiring, perhaps you can find an electronically inclined friend or a guitar repairman to make this modification for you. Exercise caution when soldering—always wear eye protection in case the solder splatters. Also, *never* use acid-core solder. It will corrode wires, pots, and anything else it contacts. Use a good electronics-grade solder that is labeled "rosin-core" (it is often labeled 60/40, as well, indicating its tin/lead ratio).

When the transformation is complete, test for correct pickup phasing: The blend of the two pickups should be louder than either pickup alone—this means that they are in phase. If the blend is softer (meaning that the pickups are out of phase), reverse the wiring of one pickup.

Some optional changes requiring the purchase of new, inexpensive parts involve changing the fader pot (potentiometer) from a 250k ohm log-taper (also called audio-taper) to a 250k ohm linear-taper pot. This gives even more control over the blending than the stock unit. Changing the stock tone capacitor to a .022μF value yields a Jaco Pastorius-like tone. (Note: the symbol μF is an abbreviation for *microfarad*, a unit of measurement in capacitors.) Insert a .05μF capacitor between the bridge and the wire running from it to the grounding point on the tone pot. This will minimize or eliminate ground-fault shocks—the kind you get when your amp's polarity doesn't match the microphone's and you get zapped.

By Dan Armstrong

Figure 5.

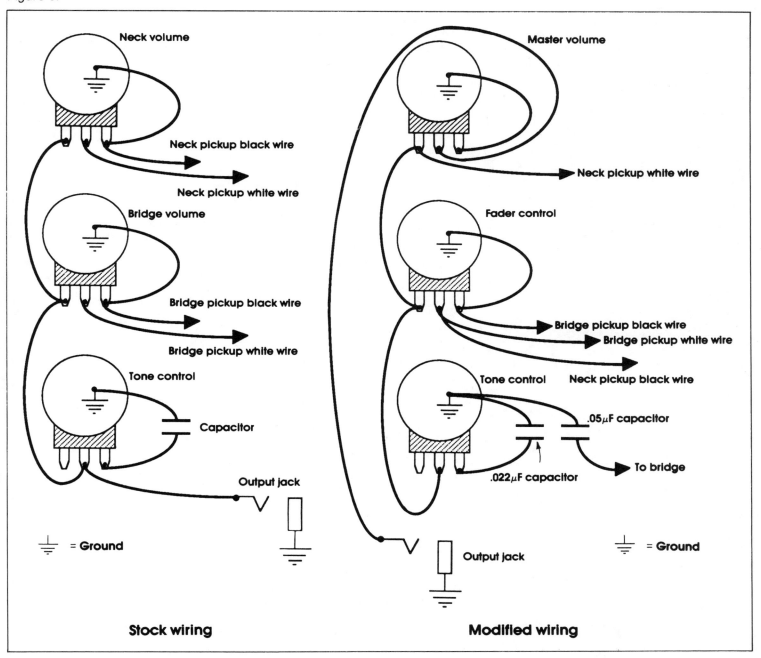

About The Authors

Dan Armstrong is a well-known designer of guitars, pickups, and effects. Ampeg's Dan Armstrong See-Through guitar and Musonics' Dan Armstrong signal processors bear his name, and he makes limited quantities of custom guitars and pickups.

Jeff Berlin is the leader of Jeff Berlin's Vox Humana, and has worked with guitarist Allan Holdsworth, drummer Bill Bruford, saxophonist Dave Liebman, and keyboardist Patrick Moraz.

Michael Brooks is a former Assistant Editor of *Guitar Player* magazine.

Bunny Brunel was born in Nice, France, but currently resides in Los Angeles, California. His extensive bass credits include work with Chick Corea, Herbie Hancock, Tony Williams, and Larry Coryell, as well as playing alongside bassist Stanley Clarke both onstage and on disc.

Stanley Clarke is one of the most popular bass guitarists in jazz history, through his solo work and his tenure with Chick Corea in Return To Forever. He is a member of *Guitar Player* magazine's Gallery Of Greats by virtue of five wins in the annual Readers Poll.

Andy Doerschuk is the Editor of GPI Special Editions, and has played drums professionally with Chet Atkins, Billy Vera and the Beaters, John Kay and Steppenwolf, guitarist Henry Kaiser, and Russian avant-garde keyboardist Sergei Kuryokhin.

Nathan East is one of the top bassists in Los Angeles, California. His credits span both the live performance and studio fields, having worked with such respected artists as Eric Clapton, Phil Collins, Kenny Loggins, and Lionel Richie.

Stuart Hamm has become a widely acclaimed bass innovator through his work with Joe Satriani and Steve Vai.

Jimmy Haslip is one of the founding members of the Yellowjackets, has performed live with Harvey Mandel, Airto Moreira, Gino Vanelli, and Dave Mason, and has recorded with Crosby, Stills & Nash, Robben Ford, and Ron Wood.

Jerry Jemmott has been playing bass for over 25 years, and has gained his reputation as a top-flight studio sideman through his work with B.B. King, Aretha Franklin, Roberta Flack, and many others.

Chris Jisi is a freelance music journalist who specializes in bass, and his work regularly appears in *Guitar Player* magazine.

Carol Kaye was one of Hollywood's premier studio bassists during the '60s and '70s. Among the many outstanding musicians she has been associated with are: Count Basie, Hampton Hawes, Roberta Flack, the Beach Boys, and Ray Charles.

Herb Mickman has studied bass with several classical teachers and with jazz bassist Charles Mingus and Scott LaFaro. He has also performed with such artists as John Coltrane, Chick Corea, Jose Feliciano, Joe Pass, Tommy Dorsey, and Barney Kessel.

Tom Mulhern is the Senior Associate Editor for *Guitar Player* magazine.

Ralph Novak has been a professional repairman for more than 18 years. He specializes in custom neck building and fretwork, and also builds guitars and basses.

Chuck Rainey has recorded and toured with a staggering number of entertainers including Ray Charles, Cannonball Adderly, Aretha Franklin, The Staples Singers, Roberta Flack, Quincy Jones, and The Crusaders.

Billy Sheehan lives in Los Angeles, California, has performed and recorded with David Lee Roth, Talas, and Tony MacAlpine, and is currently playing with his own band, Mr. Big.

Ken Smith is a 37-year-old bassist from New York who has worked professionally with big bands and numerous vocalists, among them Issac Hayes, Perry Como, and Johnny Mathis, and has played on soundtracks and commercials. He is also a teacher and builds electric basses.

From The *Guitar Player* Magazine Basic Library:

BASIC GUITAR (Revised)
Edited by Helen Casabona, Foreword by Les Paul
A completely updated edition of the most comprehensive, single-volume introduction to the technique and art of playing guitar. From the pages of *Guitar Player* magazine.
ISBN 0-88188-910-5 $14.95

ROCK GUITAR (Revised)
Edited by Helen Casabona
Carlos Santana, Eric Clapton, Lee Ritenour, Steve Morse, B.B. King, Rik Emmett, Steve Vai, Edward Van Halen, and others tell you how to get started, solo, and more. Music examples. From the pages of *Guitar Player* magazine.
ISBN 088188-908-3 $14.95

GUITAR SYNTH AND MIDI
Edited by Bradley Wait
Expand your sounds and create options with guitar synthesis. This introductory book takes you from basic concepts through advanced applications of this brave new world. From the pages of *Guitar Player* magazine.
ISBN 0-88188-593-2 $14.95

Also from GPI Books:

MASTERS OF HEAVY METAL
Edited by Jas Obrecht
"Goes to the eye of the hurricane," (Portland, Oregonian). "Fascinating!" (Newark Star Ledger). For fans and players of the immensely powerful, hugely popular, hard-core rock and roll style: intense, high-energy, guitar-dominated. Including serious, informative interviews with Jimi Hendrix, Eddie Van Halen, Jimmy Page, Randy Rhoads, Judas Priest, the Scorpions, and others. Profusely illustrated.
ISBN 0-688-02937-X $12.95

THE BIG BOOK OF BLUEGRASS
Edited by Marilyn Kochman, Foreword by Earl Scruggs
Bill Monroe, Lester Flatt, Earl Scruggs, David Grisman, Ricky Skaggs, and other popular bluegrass artists offer practical tips on playing, with note-by-note musical examples, plus valuable advice on technique and performance. The history, the greatest players, the genuine art of this authentic American commercial country folk music, more popular than ever today. Over 100 rare photos and over 50 favorite songs.
ISBN 0-688-02942-6 $12.95

GUITAR GEAR
Edited by John Brosh
A definitive guide to the instruments, accessories, gadgets, and electronic devices; the tremendous variety of both basic and sophisticated equipment that has become so crucial to the creative fulfillment of today's guitar player—how it works, how it's made, how to choose what's right for you.
ISBN 0-688-03108-0 $15.95

NEW DIRECTIONS IN MODERN GUITAR
Edited by Helen Casabona
A wealth of insight into the styles and techniques of guitarists who have moved into the vanguard of contemporary music. Artists such as Adrian Belew, Robert Fripp, Stanley Jordan, acoustic wizard Michael Hedges, and bassist Jaco Pastorius are covered in depth—with interviews, instructive musical examples, and an analysis of their playing and equipment
ISBN 0-88188-423-5 $14.95

THE GUITAR PLAYER BOOK
By the Editors of *Guitar Player* Magazine
The most comprehensive book on guitar ever produced, from the pages of America's foremost magazine for professional and amateur guitarists. Any style, any level, whether player or fan—this is the book. Includes definitive articles on all the important artists who have given the guitar its life and expression, plus design, instructions, equipment, accessories, and technique.
ISBN 0-394-62490-4 $11.95

NEW AGE MUSICIANS
Edited by Judie Eremo
The philosophy and techniques of this influential instrument style. Interviews with the foremost visionaries, including Kitaro, Will Ackerman, George Winston, and Michael Hedges. From the pages of *Guitar Player*, *Keyboard*, and *Frets* magazines.
ISBN 0-88188-909-1 $14.95

BEGINNING SYNTHESIZER
A step-by-step guide to understanding and playing synthesizers with discussions of how to use and edit presets and performance controls. A comprehensive, easy-to-understand, musical approach, with hands-on lessons in a variety of styles, including rock, pop, classical, jazz, techno-pop, blues, and more.
ISBN 0-88284-353-2 $12.95   From Alfred Publishing. (Item Number 2606.)

USING MIDI
The first comprehensive practical guide to the application of Musical Instrument Digital Interface in performance, composition, and recording, including: basic MIDI theory, using MIDI performance controls, channels and modes, sequencers, MIDI synchronization, using MIDI effects, MIDI and computers, alternate MIDI controllers, and more. A definitive and essential tutorial, from the editors of *Keyboard* magazine.
ISBN 0-88282-354-0 $12.95   From Alfred Publishing. (Item Number 2607.)